PERFORMANCE APPRAISAL
A Guide To Greater Productivity

RICHARD FISCHER OLSON

John Wiley & Sons, Inc.

New York • Chichester • Brisbane • Toronto

Library of Congress Cataloging in Publication Data

Olson, Richard Fischer.
  Performance appraisal.

  (Wiley self-teaching guides)
  Includes index.
  1. Employees,   Rating of.   I.   Title.
HF5549.5.R305   1981   658.3′125   80-29274
ISBN 0-471-09134-0

Printed in the United States of America

82   81   10 9 8 7 6 5 4 3 2 1

To Estie and Tod
My toughest appraisers

TABLE OF CONTENTS

INTRODUCTION AND ACKNOWLEDGMENT

This is a linkage book. It attempts to bridge the theoretical underpinnings of human assessment with practical, day-to-day considerations.

I write for managers who face the task of motivating others to get the job done in an ever changing work scene. The business scenario today calls for:

- Greater productivity to offset inflation and increased competition from international markets.
- A shift in emphasis from materials and budget control to managing human resources.
- Alternative forms of motivation, over and above salary and benefits.
- A partnership between boss and subordinate, in which negotiation rather than authority determines outcome.

I submit that THE PERFORMANCE APPRAISAL, one important and overlooked management tool, can provide the link between task, self motivation, and improved performance if applied intelligently.

Divided into four parts, the book traces the lineal path from appraisal to greater productivity. *Section One* looks at performance appraisal from a distance, explores it, identifies some of its pitfalls, and links its potential to productivity.

Section Two presents one model of a performance appraisal form and outlines a step-by-step process for doing an appraisal.

Section Three explores discussing the appraisal with the employee, which may have a greater impact on results than the appraisal itself.

Section Four focuses on the payoff for doing performance appraisals well—for managers, employees, and the organization.

These four sections are bracketed between a *Foreword* and an *Afterword*. The *Foreword* outlines a face-to-face appraisal in a mythical company, Metropolitan Products Incorporated (MPI)— a narrative all too close to reality. The *Afterword* rewrites the script for the same MPI performance appraisal, incorporating input from each of the four sections.

Originally, I meant to entitle this book *How Does An Appraisal Mean*? patterned after *How Does A Poem Mean*? by John Ciardi. I abandoned that tack as too obscure, but an explanation is in order. Rather than a semantic trick, I meant the title to accent the *how*, the human process that translates appraisals into a reason for action.

What is performance appraisal? I have heard systems referred to as MBO, OB Mod, Critical Incident, PF & PR, Personality Plus, WSA, Assessment Center, PMS, Work Standards, OJQ, and BARS. Forms include checklists, true-false, multiple choice, rankings, and essay items. Ratings range from 999 to 0, from outstanding to marginal, from "superstar" to "you're fired." Does all this tell you what a performance appraisal is? Of course not. Classifications facilitate memory, but not necessarily understanding.

The *what* leaves out *how* techniques are applied in the interaction between a boss and a subordinate. The feelings and emotions in that interaction dictate *how* a performance appraisal *means*, how it affects the development of the individual and the organization. I intend to show how the technical aspects of assessment can be blended with human insight to give appraisals meaning—that is, individuals feel more productive, and in fact are.

A book should come out of a rich and varied experience, but because ideas usually percolate over a period of years, it's difficult to pinpoint all the contributors. Certainly my students, colleagues and clients deserve a major share of the credit for allowing me to test concepts, make mistakes, and reconstruct my thinking in light of those errors. I am indebted to the theorists and practitioners who have been bold enough to write about evaluation. They are listed in the bibliography.

In addition, I am deeply grateful to:

— Nina Ashley, Karen Hess and Dianne Littwin for their many helpful editorial suggestions.
— My colleagues David Tronsgard and Dick Eastburn for freely reacting to the manuscript and contributing ideas of their own.
— Estie Clingman for meticulously typing and retyping the copy and proofreading the results.
— Nancy Urell for tending to the miscellany involved in researching and writing a book of this nature.
— Tod Fischer for carefully indexing important ideas and concepts.

My hope is that this book presents the state of the art, fully and accurately, while adding a perspective of its own. I have attempted to deal with the technicalities of assessment in a simple, straightforward way. This is in order to clearly demonstrate that, with deliberate skill and compassion, managers can cope with the complexities of appraisal, translating them into increased competence as well as giving employees a sense of accomplishment and worth.

Woodland
February 1981   R.F.O.

FOREWORD

"Hi, Jerry, good to see ya. Have a seat."

Jerry sits down warily.

"As you know, I called you in for your annual performance appraisal."

"No, I didn't know. Nobody told me."

"I was sure you knew. Didn't Sharon notify you?"

"I don't think so. But look, I've got ten people out there to supervise. I don't have time to read a lot of memos or attend meetings, and most of the time nobody comes out in the field to tell us what's happening."

"Well, we'll deal with that later. Let's get on with this. Do you have any questions?"

"Questions about what?"

"You know, the job and things like that."

"Well, I probably have a lot of questions, but I can't think of any right now. If I had a little time . . ."

"Well, it doesn't matter. There's no sense, you know, spending a lot of time on this thing. If you don't have any questions, I don't."

"Well, ah . . ."

"On the whole I would say it's been a pretty good year. What do you think?"

"Yeah, sure, I guess so."

"O.K. If you would just sign here, Jerry, then we can get at these computer reports to see how we're doing for the quarter."

"Ummm, what's this I'm signing?" (Jerry scans the appraisal form.)

"Oh, it's just a formality. You know, one of those ridiculous things that Personnel keeps coming up with."

"Oh, O.K." (He signs.)

(Boss sighs.) "Now that that's out of the way, let's get down to some serious business . . . ."

Record of a Performance
Appraisal of Jerry, conducted at
Metropolitan Products, Inc. (MPI).
December, 1980

"People have the capacity to go either way—toward growth or toward stagnation. The design of the system in which they work can significantly influence which way they go, and how far."

Chris Argyris

SECTION ONE:

PERFORMANCE APPRAISAL IN PERSPECTIVE

This section puts performance appraisals in perspective: relating it to productivity, delineating potential problems, and laying out a model system.

Chapter 1 brushes the dark side of appraisals, underscoring its misuses and limitations so that we might better appreciate its potentialities. Employee dissatisfaction with assessment procedures is explored, the factors many managers consider in evaluation are identified, and eighteen notions about appraisals, as commonly practiced, are postulated.

Chapter 2 draws the relationship between appraisal, the act of managing, and productivity. The elements of productivity are discussed, three reasons for doing appraisals are laid out, and EEO (Equal Employment Opportunity) issues are considered.

In Chapter 3, a model system—Performance Review and Development (PRD)—is outlined. Topics include:

— Purposes of appraisals
— Evaluation *on-the-run*
— Six elements of PRD
— Features of PRD
— Definition of terms relating to the appraisal process.

CHAPTER 1

MANAGEMENT STALEMATE OR DEVELOPMENTAL TOOL

"Evaluation is to human resource development what losing weight is to the American middle class. Nobody denies its importance . . . almost everybody has plans to do it . . . But like losing weight, the results of evaluation are rarely what one had originally hoped for." (Anthony O. Putman. "Pragmatic Evaluation," *Training and Development Journal*, October, 1980, p. 36)

Evaluating other people is a phenomenon as ancient as humankind. Societies cannot exist without judgment.

An early anecdote tells about the head monk in a monastery who called one of the novitiates before him at the end of one year of compulsory silence, to give him his end-of-year annual review.

"You have two words coming to you," opened the monk.

"Lousy food," complained the noviatiate.

"In that case, I think you'd better go back to your vow of silence for another year."

At the end of the second year, the novitiate was called in for his second annual review.

Again the monk said, "You have two words coming."

"Lumpy mattresses."

"I think you need another year of silence."

Twelve months later he was called in for his third annual review, and was allotted the usual two words.

"I quit," exclaimed the novitiate.

The head monk was reported to exclaim, "Well, it's a good thing, because all you've done since you've been here is bitch, bitch, bitch."

Apocryphal or not, the story is told to emphasize that performance appraisals are far from unique to twentieth century corporate operations. But, unlike wines, appraisals do not seem to have improved appreciably with age. The same issues remain unresolved:

— How to appraise fairly and objectively.
— How to communicate the appraisal.
— How to turn the total process into a motivator for improved performance.

Few areas of management are replete with as many contradictions and misunderstandings. The varieties of practice and results are staggering. Many reasons account for this, among them the complexity of human interaction on the job, along with the wide range of goals and methodologies. In spite of these obstacles, in order to function and grow, an organization must implement some kind of periodic assessment.

As a manager, you have two primary responsibilities:

1. To insure that the part of the organization for which you are responsible meets output objectives within quality specifications, with the optimum use of the resources at your disposal.
2. To insure maximum growth, in job knowledge and skills, of those employees who report to you.

These two accountabilities are closely related. Over the long run, high performance cannot be achieved without attention to the development of personnel. Similarly, personnel will not likely develop their potential without the challenge of high performance standards.

Periodic benchmarks help to measure the extent to which labor is divided fairly and effectively. At the same time, an appraisal system can stimulate managers toward planned actions that they might otherwise postpone or fail to accomplish.

In surveys, most managers indicate approval of performance appraisals, yet approximately half say they have never had an appraisal interview. This stands in contrast to the records showing that three-fourths of the "no-appraisals" signed forms indicating that they had such an interview, some of them several times. Were they lying? Probably not. Most likely, they had experiences similar to Jerry's (see *Foreword*). Their boss called them in and said, "How are you doing? Oh, by the way, good job this year. Would you mind signing this, and keep me posted on how our new promotion is doing. I'm going out of town—see you in a couple of weeks." In fact, they signed as a formality, with little review, and certainly with no development.

Recently, a survey of managers was conducted by the Psychological Association, Inc. of St. Louis and reported in the *Training* and *Development Journal* (October 1980, p. 7). According to the survey, over two-thirds of 360 managers in 190 organizations indicated that they:

- Do not feel their work is recognized.
- Do not get feedback on where they stand as performers.
- Do not think their superiors have adequate data for making appropriate personnel decisions.
- Rated their performance appraisal interviews from mediocre to very inadequate, as a two-way communication process.

Other significant findings in the survey include:

- 29 percent of the managers reported almost no pay-off from their last appraisal, while 40 percent were only moderately influenced.
- 79 percent indicated that data about their performance was not systematically gathered, while 52 percent reported either poorly defined procedures for recording information, or a lack of them.
- 63 percent indicated that preplanning for their performance appraisal was nonexistent.
- Most managers found that their appraisals lacked both the identification of ways to improve, and a planned followup.

To avoid results like those reported by the Psychological Association, organizations have experimented with many different programs, ranging from open-ended narratives to computerized systems, with a variety of criteria for rating employees.

Stop here to list the criteria you use in evaluating your employees. What performance factors are most important to you? Rank them in order of importance, e.g., most important first, etc.

1.

2.

3.

4.

5.

6.

7.

8.

9.

10.

The Conference Board studied appraisal systems from 125 companies. (The results were reported by Robert I. Lazer and Walter S. Wikstrom in *Appraising Managerial Performance: Current Practices and Future Directions*, The Conference Board, Inc., New York, 1977.) Here are some of the terms appearing on appraisal forms from 61 of the firms. The number of companies rating a particular factor appears in parentheses. Compare your criteria to theirs.

- Knowledge of work (49)
- Leadership (38)
- Initiative (38)
- Quality of work (37)
- Quantity of work (34)
- Cooperation (34)
- Judgment (33)
- Creativity (31)
- Dependability (31)
- Planning (27)
- Communication (23)
- Intelligence (22)
- Problem solving (19)
- Delegation (19)
- Attitude (18)
- Motivation and effort (15)
- Organization (14)

You may have listed only a few of these factors, since they represent personality traits or traditional management functions. Unless converted to specific job behavior, they tend to be subjective.

Many organizations (yours may be included) use other criteria for evaluating employees, such as objectives, job behavior, and the like. In MBO (Management by Objective), managers, and sometimes subordinates, set objectives and measure progress toward them. MBO has failed to meet expectations because: managers do not know how to involve subordinates; they frequently set simplistic objectives that can easily be measured and reached; and they tie the assessment of those objectives directly to compensation.

Behavioral scaling is a process that requires identifying successful behaviors on the job and scaling them. Managers rate subordinates on that list of predetermined behaviors. Its aim is to remove assessor bias by providing preset criteria. Its success is undetermined at this time. (An example of a behaviorally anchored rating scale (BARS) appears in Chapter 7.)

Whatever the system, procedure or criteria, certain common problems persist. Before reading on, look at assessment as it is used in your organization, and think of all the problems you've experienced. Consider failings and inadequate procedures. List the five major difficulties you encounter:

1.

2.

3.

4.

5.

A group of managers identified the following problems with appraisals. Contemplate your answers in light of their list:

— Unclear, confusing, and sometimes complex procedures
— Lack of skill in appraising
— Lack of management commitment and support
— Subjective, non-job-related criteria
— Compensation oriented, rather than developmental
— Lack of continuing assessment throughout the year, and from year to year
— Politically influenced
— Failure to give negative feedback
— Demotivating effect (subordinates react defensively to criticism, which sometimes adversely affects future performance)
— Lack of reliability (ratings not replicable across evaluators)
— Lack of validity (ratings do not predict successful job performance)
— Individual goals conflicting with unit, group or departmental goals

— Confusion between methods and results
— Difficulty in weighing judgmental areas of performance (vs. the clearly measurable)
— Lack of preparation
— Discomfort with involving subordinates in a two-way process
— Inability to handle disagreement or emotional reactions
— An excessively time-consuming process
— Little reward for doing effective appraisals
— Failure to contribute to production

Despite these problems, appraisal systems persist, probably because of the belief that, with a formal process, managers are more likely to make verifiable evaluations that are representative of a subordinate's overall performance. A sanctioned system emphasizes careful judgment rather than hunch.

To further illuminate the gap between hopes for performance appraisal and its historical shortcomings, the second half of this chapter challenges your thinking with a series of observations from the literature and from my experience with organizations. Before you consider these observations, indicate agreement or disagreement with the following statements by circling the appropriate number.

	Strongly Disagree	Tend to Disagree	Tend to Agree	Strongly Agree
1. Ratings are necessary to develop subordinates.	1	2	3	4
2. Subordinates prefer a boss who gives them the answers.	1	2	3	4
3. Most subordinates know what is expected.	1	2	3	4
4. Politics has no place in performance appraisals.	1	2	3	4
5. Bosses like to play God when appraising performance.	1	2	3	4

	Strongly Disagree	Tend to Disagree	Tend to Agree	Strongly Agree
6. Appraisals should be used to determine compensation.	1	2	3	4
7. Appraisals motivate employees to perform better.	1	2	3	4
8. Criticism doesn't bother top employees.	1	2	3	4
9. Subordinates should be given a copy of their appraisal.	1	2	3	4
10. Most subordinates see the job as much more complex and demanding than it really is.	1	2	3	4
11. "How promotable an employee is" should be part of the appraisal.	1	2	3	4
12. Managers readily give negative information to subordinates.	1	2	3	4
13. Most employees would prefer not to be appraised.	1	2	3	4
14. Bosses want subordinates to speak up and disagree with them.	1	2	3	4

Keep in mind your responses as you consider the ideas that follow. These notions are based on how appraisals are generally conducted: on what is, not what ought to be. They should stimulate you to think about assessment practices in your organization. Question them; disagree with them. Test them against your experience.

NOTION 1:   RATING AN EMPLOYEE'S PERFORMANCE IS FREQUENTLY ANTITHETICAL TO DEVELOPING THAT PERFORMANCE.

Ratings are a small part of assessment, yet frequently an all–pervasive one. Like grades in school, ratings tend to stifle action and encourage reaction. Employees play it close to the vest by doing only what earns them good ratings, not necessarily what will improve job performance. They quickly learn "what the teacher wants" and behave accordingly. If ratings are average or below, employees may actually walk away with the attitude of "why try because it doesn't make any difference anyway, "Because appraisals present no image of an improved future they often demotivate. They dwell on the past and lack direction or support. Usually subordinates are left to flounder on their own.

Second guessing is a luxury of gods, Monday morning quarterbacks and bosses. There is no dignity in negative criticism. Critiquing a performance is painful, unless, of course, the accomplishments deserve only accolades. All the more reason why evaluation should be handled skillfully and sensitively.

NOTION 2:   APPRAISING PERFORMANCE TO DETERMINE COMPENSATION IS NOT THE SAME AS APPRAISING PERFORMANCE TO DEVELOP EMPLOYEES.

Most performance appraisal systems are used for salary purposes. Typically, the Personnel department sends a memo to a manager saying that "Henderson" is due for a raise and an appraisal is needed for the record. Then the manager decides how much to pay Henderson, fills out a form to justify the raise, and sends it back to Personnel. In short, the appraisal is completed to substantiate a pay hike, rather than improve Henderson's performance.

COROLLARY: AN APPRAISAL REPORTING SYSTEM IS NOT THE SAME AS AN APPRAISAL FOR DEVELOPMENT.

Sometimes managers associate an effective performance appraisal system with elaborate forms and numerical reports, due twice a year in triplicate. Developing subordinates is related more to systematic procedures and understanding, than to a large volume of paperwork and numerical addition.

NOTION 3:   MOST PERFORMANCE APPRAISALS ARE BASED ON SUBJECTIVE CRITERIA.

Note how many of the criteria that showed up in the Conference Board survey (see page 6) lack definition, concreteness, and measurability. Too often appraisers are swayed by how likeable employees are, and if they do "what they are told."

NOTION 4: FREQUENTLY MANAGERS AND EMPLOYEES DO NOT SEE A JOB IN THE SAME WAY, EVEN THOUGH THE MANAGERS ASSUME EMPLOYEES KNOW WHAT IS EXPECTED.

Common sense tells us that subordinates know our expectations. But then, common sense also told us that the earth was flat and the center of the universe.

FIRST COROLLARY: JOB DESCRIPTIONS ARE USUALLY AN INADEQUATE, OUTDATED INDICATOR OF JOB EXPECTATIONS.

Most often job descriptions are job straitjackets. They are:

— Usually devised by somebody "up there" with little input from those who perform or manage the job.
— Ideal conceptions of the job with little resemblance to reality.
— General in nature, without specifying actual tasks and behavior.
— Seldom revised to reflect changes in the job.
— Seldom read, discussed or used in any meaningful way.

Of course, there are exceptions. Some organizations use job descriptions that are running accounts of work specifications and serve as the basis for reaching agreement on management expectations.

SECOND COROLLARY: THE CLOSER ONE IS TO A JOB, THE MORE UNPREDICTABLE AND DEMANDING IT IS.

From the manager's view, the employee's job is generally clear-cut and easily accomplished: "I just tell 'em exactly how to do it." From the employee's viewpoint, the job is demanding and unpredictable. Call this the *principle of propinquity*. Nearness to the actual work can cause disagreement over evaluating the work. Bosses see bits and pieces from afar. They judge highlights like skimming the chapter headings in a book. Employees experience the day-to-day frustrations, the nuances of a job, and tend to have a nearsighted view of work. The ancient refrain about the forest and the tree states the *principle of propinquity*.

THIRD COROLLARY: EMPLOYEES SAY MANAGERS ARE TOO FAR REMOVED FROM THE JOB TO ASSESS IT, YET IF THEY SUPERVISE MORE CLOSELY, THEY ARE VIEWED AS NIT-PICKING AND LACKING OBJECTIVITY.

This is the *Catch 22* of managing. How can bosses know what's going on without looking over the employee's shoulder? Resolution of this dilemma places greater importance on multiple sources of information and on periodic dialogues about performance.

NOTION 5:   MOST APPRAISALS ARE NOT COMMUNICATED TO EMPLOYEES IN A MEANINGFUL WAY.

As indicated earlier, most managers do not discuss appraisals with their subordinates. If they do, it is accomplished in a hurried, offhand, cursory fashion—a duty downplayed to a non-essential management activity. *Communicating appraisals to employees is probably more important than the appraisal itself.* Of course, if appraisals are used chiefly for determining compensation, there is no great need to communicate. The employee's check will say it all. Sometimes the manager doesn't even know when raises become effective, or how much the raise will be. In appraising for development, it's impossible to avoid a dialogue with employees, even though managers are unaccustomed to it.

COROLLARY: BOSSES USUALLY DO NOT GIVE NEGATIVE FEEDBACK.

When they sit on the assessor's throne, managers find it's not easy playing God. They must work with the employee the next day. Why be too negative? Hence, a lack of accomplishment tends to be glossed over in an effort to avoid unpleasantness. Except, of course, in a crisis: then negatives take the form of hellfire and brimstone, and are so intense that subordinates usually discard whatever truth is in them. If mishandled, negative feedback can cause lasting resentment.

NOTION 6:   MOST APPRAISALS ARE CONSIDERED ONCE-A-YEAR EVENTS RATHER THAN ONGOING PROCESSES.

Managers have difficulty feeling comfortable sitting down with subordinates once a year to assess performance. This method begs for accumulated frustrations and misunderstandings. Employees can't correct deficiencies they don't recognize. Day to day, week to week, and month to month communication can have a greater impact on performance than the annual interview.

NOTION 7:   MOST PERFORMANCE APPRAISALS ARE UNRELIABLE.

Studies substantiate that if different managers evaluate the same performance, they come up with a range of ratings. Most assessments are not duplicated by other managers, and hence are *unreliable*. If unstable, decisions based on appraisals are risky and uncertain.

NOTION 8:   MOST PERFORMANCE APPRAISALS ARE INVALID.

Again, studies suggest that ratings do not necessarily correlate with actual job performance. Another way of saying it is: do high performance appraisal ratings insure job success? Usually the answer is no.

The next eight notions offer a partial explanation for the lack of reliability and validity in the appraisal process.

NOTION 9: APPRAISING PERFORMANCE IS FREQUENTLY A POLITICAL PROCESS.

What superiors want affects the way managers assess employees. In fairness to the employee, managers should negotiate with their superiors prior to conducting formal appraisal interviews. Some subordinates learn how to influence ratings by "pleasing the boss."

NOTION 10: THE POLICIES AND TRADITIONS OF THE DEPARTMENT INFLUENCE APPRAISALS.

Some departments insist that all employees are above average, and their ratings are skewed upward. Others implement a tight policy of "dangling the carrot." For instance, manufacturing managers tend to be tough graders, while marketing managers are high markers. Organizations also differ in their attitude toward disclosure, ranging from secrecy to open discussion about performance.

NOTION 11: ASSESSING PERFORMANCE IS INFLUENCED BY FORCES OUTSIDE THE ORGANIZATION.

Pressure from unions, customers, EEOC (the Equal Employment Opportunity Commission), OSHA (Occupational Safety and Health Administration), and economic turndowns influence the way managers assess performance. EEO, as discussed in Chapters 2 and 6, can force managers to become more explicit about the job and standards of performance.

NOTION 12: PROMOTABILITY INFLUENCES PERFORMANCE APPRAISALS.

Most performance appraisal forms include a section for managers not only to estimate the employee's promotability, but also to suggest a timetable. Many follow the rule that employees cannot be *outstanding* unless they are promotable. This practice raises serious questions about the relationship between performance and promotability, and to what extent they should relate. What about the career salesperson or supervisor? Shouldn't they be able to receive top ratings?

NOTION 13: A CENTRAL TENDENCY PERSISTS TO RATE EVERYONE "ABOVE AVERAGE."

Managers hesitate to discriminate between employees, preferring to ride a middle-of-the-road, positively slanted track. Hence, most merit systems are *merit* in name only. Managers lean toward the center because they:

— Want employees to get the best possible raise.
— Have to work day-to-day with employees *after* the performance appraisals.
— May have to communicate the ratings face to face.
— Are not confident in the validity of their ratings.
— Cannot provide tangible evidence to support negative assessments.
— Assume employees prefer it that way.

NOTION 14:   EVEN WHEN APPRAISAL CRITERIA ARE SPECIFIED, THE WEIGHT GIVEN EACH CRITERION IS NOT.

For instance, how does keeping a neat working space stack up against meeting production quotas? This may seem like a strange question, but a district manager once told me he had a top sales representative who kept such a sloppy car that every time the manager traveled with him, he found the car predominated his opinion of that rep. The manager became so obsessed with the mess that he ignored the accomplishments of the rep. Finally in exasperation he commanded: "Clean up the car so I can get on with my managing!" And the rep did.

The DM overtly weighted the criterion of tidiness, even though it is easy to disagree with its importance.

NOTION 15:   CURRENT EVENTS TAKE PRECEDENCE OVER PAST.

"What have you done for me lately!" In the pennant stretch, past accomplishments are easily forgotten. The question is how many hits and RBI's did the player have today? Since appraisal tends to be an annual affair (Notion 6), managers very often systematically ignore performance data for the first part of a year and respond to year end accomplishments or failures.

NOTION 16:   PROGRAMED ACTIVITIES TAKE PRECEDENCE OVER UNPROGRAMED.

Think back to school days. What subjects did you work on daily and which ones did you let slide? Daily, visible requirements, like math and foreign language assignments, were usually tended to fairly diligently. Long-term activites such as research papers, novels, reviews, and projects, were allowed to drift until 48 hours before the due date. Like students, managers probably focus on the day-to-day tangibles that can be readily measured, and devote less attention to planning, developing surbordinates, and other important, but less discernible, management behaviors.

NOTION 17:   LACK OF PARTICIPATION BY EMPLOYEES IN THEIR APPRAISALS IS ASSOCIATED WITH A LACK OF

STATUS AND CREDIBILITY OF THE PERFORMANCE APPRAISAL SYSTEM.

Most studies strongly indicate that a commitment to performance appraisal is directly related to involvement in all aspects of the system. (Chapter 11 examines employee participation in greater detail.)

NOTION 18: AN ORGANIZATION'S ABILITY TO DESIGN PERFORMANCE APPRAISAL SYSTEMS OUTSTRIPS ITS IMPLEMENTATION SKILLS.

The bottom line is application. Does assessing performance lead to increased productivity? Does it help or hinder the employee? The manager? Does it contribute to the mission of the organization?

1. Ratings frequently work against, not for, employee development.
2. Appraising for compensation is not the same as appraising for development.
3. Performance appraisals tend to be subjective.
4. Boss and subordinate frequently assume agreement on what is expected, when little agreement actually exists.
5. Most performance appraisals are not communicated in any meaningful way to employees.
6. Appraisal is a once-a-year event, rather than an on-going process.
7. Most performance appraisals are unreliable.
8. Most performance appraisals are invalid.
9. Politics influences appraisals.
10. Departmental policy and procedures affect appraisals.
11. Outside forces touch the appraisal process.
12. "Promotability" impacts on appraisals.
13. Managers tend to rate everyone "above average."
14. Most appraisal systems do not specify the weight given each criterion.
15. Current performance takes precedence over past.
16. Programed acts take precedence over unprogramed.
17. Low employee participation in appraisals usually is related to the low status and credibility of the system.
18. The ability to design appraisal systems outstrips the ability to implement them.

SUMMARY OF NOTIONS ABOUT PERFORMANCE APPRAISALS

All these observations will be treated in depth in succeeding chapters that focus on implementation:

HOW do you do a performance appraisal?
HOW do you translate the appraisal into improved job performance?

In effect,

HOW does a performance appraisal mean?

SO PERFORMANCE APPRAISAL: MANAGEMENT STALEMATE OR DEVELOPMENTAL TOOL?

The 18 notions answer the question. Despite good intentions, most appraisals fall short of expectations and in some cases are fiascos. Most organizations use ratings to determine numerical position on a salary scale, but there are few examples of appraisal for employee development.

Yes, assessment *is* difficult, for reasons cited in this chapter. We do not like our contributions downgraded, even when the evaluator is right. But assessment as a developmental tool is possible. The success of performance appraisals, whatever system is used, depends on:

- Top management's active support
- Training in appraisal skills
- Goal orientation (rather than reliance on traits or characteristics)
- Separation from compensation
- A continuing process (not a once-a-year ritual)

Transforming assessment into a management tool for developing people constitutes the theme of this book. Succeeding chapters present a step-by-step refresher if you are a veteran appraiser, and an orientation if you are a new manager. As a developmental process, appraising performance involves the form, data and mechanics of interaction between the protagonists: the supervisor and those supervised. The aim of the game is *productivity*, the topic of the next chapter.

A NOTE ABOUT THE APPLICATION AND REVIEW ACTIVITIES AT THE END OF EACH CHAPTER:

These activities are designed to link your work experience with the ideas in this book, by helping you organize key concepts and stimulate your thinking about your appraisal practices. To gain maximum benefit from this book, complete the activities before proceeding to the next chapter.

APPLICATION AND REVIEW

1. Indicate to what extent you agree or disagree with the following statements by checking one of the 4 responses to the right:

	Strongly Disagree	Tend to Disagree	Tend to Agree	Strongly Agree
	1	2	3	4
a. Managers should conduct formal performance appraisals with each subordinate at least twice a year.				
b. Our current performance appraisal system is an effective way to develop subordinates.				
c. Subordinates should participate in setting their performance goals.				
d. Managers should ask for a self-evaluation from subordinates before they formulate their rating.				
e. Managers should tell subordinates their rating.				
f. Managers should discuss every aspect of the performance appraisal with subordinates.				
g. Appraising performance ranks with planning and organizing as an important management function.				
h. Most performance appraisals are subjective.				
i. Managers frequently recognize subordinates for their good work.				
j. Subordinates want the boss to tell them when they are not doing well.				
k. Our current performance appraisal system is viewed by subordinates as being fair.				
l. Subordinates should be appraised by more than one person.				
m. My last performance appraisal conducted by my superior was accurate and competently done.				

2. a. When was the last time your performance was assessed and discussed with you?

   b. Should it be done more frequently? Less frequently?

   c. What do you wish your superior would do differently when assessing you?

   d. Relate your answers in a, b and c to the frequency and method by which you assess your employees.

3. What type of criteria do you use in your current appraisal system?
   _____ Traits (sincerity, enthusiasm, maturity, etc.)
   _____ Management tasks (organizing, planning, motivating, etc.)
   _____ List of job behaviors (gives clear, well-prepared presentations; recognizes others for work well done; follows company policies and procedures, etc.)
   _____ Goals (achieve 32 percent of the market share on "Big D" deodorant, establish a new cost savings program for the Riverton plant, etc.)

   Check the appropriate items above and list the advantages and disadvantages of your system in the space below.

Advantages	Disadvantages

4. Compare your responses on pp. 8–9 to the 18 notions.

   (a) Would you change any response(s)? _____

(b) Which of the notions do you disagree with?

Nos. _____

_____

(c) Which surprised you?

Nos. _____

_____

(d) Which are the most difficult to deal with in your appraisals?

Nos. _____

_____

SUGGESTED RESPONSES

1. Compare your answers to 350 managers who have responded to this Performance Appraisal Survey. Their mean scores were:

a.	3.1	h.	3.0
b.	1.5	i.	2.7
c.	3.4	j.	2.4
d.	2.1	k.	2.0
e.	3.5	l.	2.9
f.	3.9	m.	2.8
g.	3.2		

Generally managers:

— Do not feel comfortable letting subordinates rate themselves.
— Probably do not praise subordinates enough.
— Are not sure subordinates want to hear negative feedback.
— Feel one person—the boss—should rate a subordinate.
— Believe that all aspects of appraisals, including the rating, should be discussed with employees.
— Agree that subordinates should participate in setting performance goals.
— Consider their appraisal systems ineffective in developing subordinates.
— Feel most subordinates consider appraisals unfair.
— Do not believe *they* are being accurately and competently assessed by their superiors.

CHAPTER 2

APPRAISAL
AND PRODUCTIVITY

Chapter 1 outlined problems involved in conducting effective performance appraisals. This chapter explains why mounting economic pressures, changing human needs and recent government mandates are prompting many managers to take a fresh look at their appraisal systems.

The Organizational Control diagram shows the organization's need for a systematic way to direct its activities. I prefer to depict the organization on its side, the hierarchy (triangle) preserved, so that the *thrust* (production line or face-to-face with customers) is *out* there rather than *down* there. Top management determines the mission, then organizes human, fiscal, and technological resources around a structure bolstered by policies and tradition.

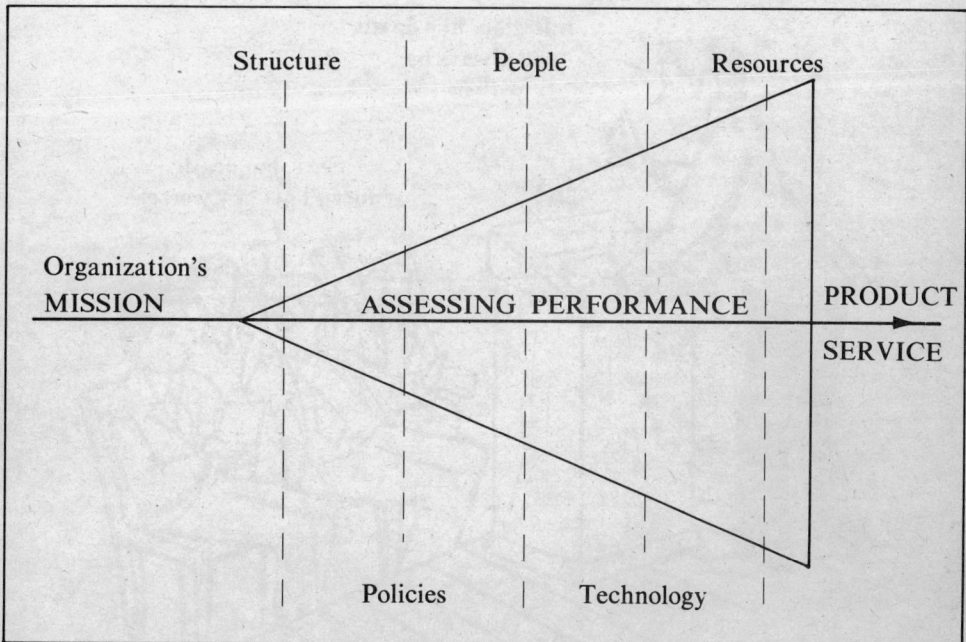

Structure　　　People　　　Resources

Organization's
MISSION　　　　ASSESSING PERFORMANCE　　PRODUCT

SERVICE

Policies　　　Technology

**Organizational Control Through
Performance Appraisal**

To realize its mission, an organization must monitor the performance of its members. This is accomplished primarily through a methodology of:

- Assigning work to people
- Determining the criteria for judging the quality of the work
- Inspecting the work
- Measuring the results against established criteria
- Taking corrective action based on the assessment.

Evaluation plays a dual role in the control process: it is fundamental to regulating current performance and provides the base for establishing new standards and goals.

Three reasons why managers should reexamine their appraisal practices are:

— The organization's need to increase productivity
— The individual's need to know
— The government's involvement through social legislation

THE ORGANIZATION'S NEED
TO INCREASE PRODUCTIVITY

Though I don't hold to absolutes, I am resigned to live with certain *persistents*. Inflation is one.

Newspapers and business journals present gloomy forecasts by economy-watchers. Books on *how to survive bad times* outsell *Paradise Lost, Alice In Wonderland* and *Lost Horizons*. Every ten years we expect to find the dollar worth one-half of what it was during the previous decade. (We can take solace in the ancient riddle about "halving." At least the dollar will never reach zero.) One hedge for organizations against the sledgehammer effects of inflation is to optimize their resources and increase production.

The following equation outlines a simple way to understand productivity:

$$\text{PRODUCTIVITY} = \frac{\text{OUTPUT}}{\text{INPUT}}$$

Output is the product or service delivered by the organization, and input includes capital (facilities, machines, equipment), materials (raw and otherwise), energy, and labor.

For example, if MPI (Metropolitan Products Inc., the hypothetical corporation mentioned in the *Foreword*) sold and collected $1,000,000,000 worth of goods in 1981, and paid out $800,000,000 in capital, materials, energy, and labor, their productivity could be described by the ratio $\frac{10}{8}$ or $\frac{5}{4}$ or 1.25. If, in 1982, sales remain at $1,000,000,000 and costs escalate to $900,000,000, then MPI's productivity would decline to $\frac{10}{9}$ or 1.11. To increase productivity, management must add sales, reduce costs, or both.

Of course it's not as simple as that. Unstable international conditions in the oil-producing Mideast make it difficult to project energy costs. A more complex issue is how to quantify the employees' contribution to an increase in production or a reduction in costs.

Measuring productivity is one problem. Increasing it is another. (In the 21st century, I suspect we will find more and more reason to support a "minimum growth" society, but that is a topic for other books, in another time and place.) Organizations must contend with the following factors:

External Conditions

   a) Spiraling costs—labor, energy, technology, raw materials.
   b) Fewer investments in tools and resources for production because of the growing stockpile of government regulations, the shrinkage in retained earnings, etc.
   c) Labor producing less—the shift from manufacturing to services, an inexperienced and more diverse labor force, less emphasis on the work ethic.

Internal Conditions

   a) Lack of in-company controls, e.g. an effective performance appraisal system.
   b) Failure to tap the wisdom of the workers.

c) Failure to systematically remove impediments to productivity, including:
— Lack of faith in workers
— History of distrust between management and labor
— Lack of knowledge and understanding
— Improper supervision
— Union or industry norms for mediocre performance
— Lack of skills training at all levels
— A work force that conforms less and complains more

Over the last 150 years, efforts to cope with the internal conditions affecting productivity have clustered into five approaches:

Slave Labor. The graphic examples of worker exploitation involved blacks, children, and migrants—all extreme measures for keeping labor costs down.

The Cult of Efficiency. In the 1920s and 30s there was a strong movement to tighten up, to reduce input costs through time/method studies, standard operating procedures, equipment design, and by engineering people as well as machines.

The Suggestion Box. In its simplest form, a wooden container placed near the time clock inviting employee ideas. More often than not, the suggestions were unprintable. The most comprehensive approach is the Scanlon Plan, which sets up committees throughout the organization to evaluate employee proposals for improvement and to award compensation for successful suggestions, based on a formula related to production and profits. One side-effect of the committees is the improvement of team-work between management and labor.

Quality of Work Life (QWL). QWL stems from the human relations movement of the post-Depression era. Efforts were made to change the work environment along with management-employee relationships, thereby increasing worker satisfaction and the motivation to produce. Some current programs extend the QWL concept by allowing employees to set their own hours, work procedures, and production standards.

Pride in Work. A composite approach emphasizing that ideas, like cars, should be pooled. *Quality Circles* is one such program, in which managers and workers are trained in trouble shooting and problem solving. They work in ad hoc teams, creating alternate solutions to specific production problems. PRIDE (used here as a catch phrase for Productivity in Response to Interactive Development of Employees) recognizes that, as society becomes more complex and as organizations grow, jobs become more specialized and compartmentalized. The average employee feels less and less a part of the organization. PRIDE theorizes that, by giving supervisors and workers a chance to interact and to develop their attitudes and work habits, production will be increased and/or cost savings will be realized.

Whatever method managers use to increase productivity, they need a delivery system. Performance appraisal is a natural medium for translating ideas into action.

THE INDIVIDUAL'S NEED TO KNOW

In a recent survey conducted among 8,524 employees of a large corporation, the majority of respondents indicated that:

- The company was losing touch with its employees
- Supervisors did not communicate ways to grow and did not assist workers in developing their careers.

This is a second reason for upgrading appraisal efforts. At all levels (see survey above) employees want to know:

- What is expected?
- How am I doing?
- Where am I going?
- How can I improve?
  And, of course, most important,
- What will be the reward for improving?

All generations have demanded greater control over their lives. (Compare your demands with those of your parents and those of your children.)

A source of much of the unrest in the 60s was youth's impatience with policies, rules and regulations set by others. In the 70s, many employees insisted on more information, and on more two-way communication. They wanted to know the *why*'s of policies and procedures, especially those that affected their careers. By 1980, five states had followed the precedent of the federal government's Privacy Act of 1974 by passing their own laws. These made it mandatory that employees have access to their personnel records, including appraisals. Since *disclosure* will likely be the trend of the 80s, managers ought to take greater care in preparing and conducting appraisals.

GOVERNMENT'S INVOLVEMENT THROUGH SOCIAL LEGISLATION

In 1970, the Equal Employment Opportunity Commission (EEOC) issued *Guidelines on Employee Selection Procedures,* followed in June, 1978, by a revised *Uniform Guidelines on Employee Selection Procedures.* The new edict includes performance appraisal procedures, as well as employment selection. It covers all decisions involving hiring, promotion, retention, demotion, transfer, and referral.

One of the early court cases that led to the new guidelines was *Albermarle vs. Moody (1975),* in which an employer tried to defend the use of a personnel screening instrument, saying it was based on supervisory ratings. The court found that supervisors' ratings are frequently unreliable and inconsistent. (Chapter 6 summarizes important court cases that relate to the appraisal process. Also see Dena B. Schneier's "The Impact of EEO Legislation on Performance Appraisals" in *Personnel,* July-August, 1978.)

Over the past decade, the courts have ruled that employee ratings are discriminatory when:

— Based on subjective or ill-defined criteria, rather than on a job analysis.
— Data on which they are based is not collected and scored under standardized conditions.
— Unvalidated.
— They result in disparate rejection rates—that is, white, middle class males are promoted while women and members of minority groups are rejected.

Performance appraisal practices are necessary and essential to the safe and efficient conduct of one's business. In addition, the organization must demonstrate that no other system would be less discriminatory than the one in effect. Finally, appraisals must be valid; they must accurately measure significant aspects of the job.

Some managers consider EEO an intrusion on management prerogatives, but, in effect, EEO forces them to become more explicit about how they select and manage employees. Like it or not, EEO creates more attention for performance appraisals.

The three—productivity, the employee's need for information, and EEO considerations—are interrelated. Inventing new procedures and technologies necessary to increase productivity requires that managers:

• Seek better sources of data.
• Document their successes and failures.
• Improve the quality of their communication with employees.
• Search out the knowledge and experience of employees.
• Make better-informed and unbiased judgments.
• Become more explicit about the goals of the organization and of their departments.

Before we fill in the gaps in the appraisal-productivity relationship, write your definition of *management* below:

However you explain managing, your definition probably includes one or more of the following elements:

— Deciding on the task
— Dividing labor
— Setting targets
— Measuring progress
— Reacting promptly when targets are not met.

Certainly you do these tasks whether or not they are explicitly stated. Compare them to the monitoring process outlined at the beginning of this chapter.

Assessing performance involves activities that are integral to managing, label them what you will. If your unit, your department, your organization are to continue to grow, organizational goals must be translated into formulations relevant to each employee. All goals must be periodically monitored and updated; subordinates should be helped to achieve them, and the results should be assessed. The following diagram suggests the relationship between performance appraisals and increased productivity.

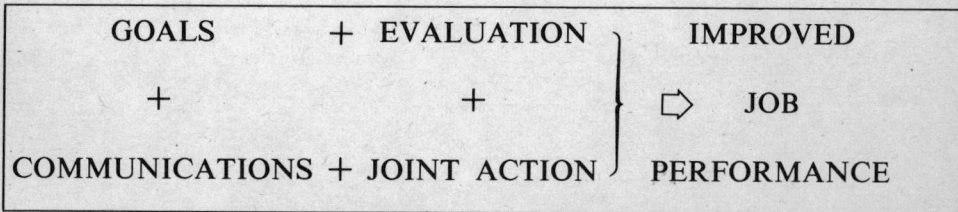

```
| GOALS          + EVALUATION ┐    IMPROVED
|                             |
|     +               +       ├─⇨  JOB
|                             |
| COMMUNICATIONS + JOINT ACTION ┘   PERFORMANCE
```

In any formal group such as a corporation, the members need to know where they are going (GOALS). Information must be exchanged (COMMUNICATIONS) about the goals and processes to achieve them. At regular intervals, procedures and results need to be looked at

(EVALUATION), in order to substantiate their relevance, practicality and impact. Involving team members (JOINT ACTION) in this system enhances the system's chances of success (IMPROVED JOB PERFORMANCE).

In terms of conditions internal to an organization and under its control, productivity is related above all to human resources. Organizations have yet to begin tapping the potential of their employees. (For that matter, you and I probably have achieved no more than 20 percent of our capabilities). Since raw material, equipment and labor costs will, most likely, continue to soar, the critical focus of any productivity effort is on people. Organizations need to find the mechanism for helping employees increase their output or decrease the cost of procedures, operations and systems (input).

Job failures are seldom due to a lack of technical know-how, but too often result from the inability of well-intentioned people to function together. Most managers pay lip service to making people more productive (and the business more efficient and effective), but few know how to go about it or how to measure the human factor in the equation. Performance appraisal, as discussed in the next chapter, forces managers to set targets and specify ways to measure results.

Your performance appraisal system, then, is a key mechanism for battling decreasing productivity and profits. The way you and your colleagues implement appraisals is more critical than the system itself. A loosely structured system implemented by skilled, committed managers can be successful; conversely, super-computerized systems administered by untrained, uncaring managers will , most likely, produce inconsequential results.

Chapter 3 outlines the elements of a sound appraisal program. The rest of the book covers implementation: the strategy and tactics for stimulating greater productivity.

APPLICATION AND REVIEW

1. Give 3 reasons for doing performance appraisals:

    (a)

    (b)

    (c)

2. What are the essential elements of the appraisal process?

3. List 4 reasons why performance ratings may be considered discriminatory:

    (a)

    (b)

    (c)

    (d)

4. List two things you can do to:

    (a) Better inform employees of their progress (or lack of it)

    (b) More adequately comply with EEO guidelines

    (c) Relate performance appraisal to productivity (Output/Input)

SUGGESTED RESPONSES

1. Increase productivity, keep employees informed, and meet EEO guidelines.
2. Goals, criteria, performance information, measurement, communication, evaluation, and joint action.
3. Subjective, biased, not standardized, unvalidated.
4. Responses will vary.

CHAPTER 3

PERFORMANCE REVIEW AND DEVELOPMENT: WHAT IS IT?

To upgrade evaluative processes, organizations and managers need to ask:

- How should we appraise?
- How should we communicate appraisals?
- How often should we communicate?
- How can we convert appraisals into personnel development?
- How can we translate development into greater productivity?

To answer some of these questions, this chapter presents an appraisal process called PERFORMANCE REVIEW AND DEVELOPMENT or PRD. A true appraisal includes review *and* development, in which boss and subordinate look at how things are going and plan future work based on their joint view.

PRD is represented here as a model process for your examination. Compare it to the appraisal system you are currently using.

The objectives of PRD (or any appraisal system, for that matter) are to help managers:

- Identify the key requirements of the job and develop a mutual understanding of responsibilities and goals at three levels: the employee being evaluated, the appraiser, and the appraiser's superior.
- Evaluate an employee's performance as objectively as possible, against specified job goals.
- Provide the basis for improving job performance by:
  - Identifying specific areas for employee improvement.
  - Developing a mutually agreed-upon plan to improve the employee's performance.
  - Providing support and specific feedback to the employee, increasing the probability that performance will improve.
  - Gaining commitment and involvement from employees.
- Provide a flow of information about the performance and developmental needs of employees, to enhance future personnel decisions about

job assignments, promotions, transfers, and terminations.
- Achieve greater use of employee skills and capabilities, directly (and indirectly) influencing productivity.

These objectives frame an environment conducive to developing human potential. Left out is salary administration. Every organization works to provide an equitable and competitive compensation program. Unfortunately, appraisals get caught between development and remuneration. (See Notion 2 in Chapter 1.) Consider what happens.

When appraising for salary purposes, managers inflate ratings and minimize failings to obtain acceptable raises for their employees. Knowing their ratings will determine next year's salary, employees are less receptive to admitting their inadequacies. Linking appraisals to job improvement requires an open and honest dialogue about accomplishments and lack of accomplishment.

How do we resolve the incompatibility? At present, total separation of PRD from compensation is unrealistic. Most appraisals (including yours, I suspect) enter into salary decisions. I suggest that we minimize the dual purpose by treating appraisal as a continuing activity. Think of it this way: you will spend approximately 200 hours (100, 300, whatever) with each subordinate during the year. What's the best use of that time? That is quite a different question from: how will you conduct the year-end review?

| January | March | June | September | December |

A Continuum of Manager-Exployee Interaction

The small dots on the Continuum of Manager-Employee Interaction represent week-to-week contact with subordinates (meetings, project analyses, day-to-day interactions). The large ones represent formal sessions for setting goals (January) and the year-end performance appraisal interview. Between are quarterly progress reviews.

At first glance, you're probably thinking, "I don't have enough time." I would argue that the continuity concept doesn't demand *more* time, but better use of time. Instead of cramming at the last minute for the annual review, you would take advantage of any interaction with a subordinate, whether five minutes or five hours, to gather performance data, praise competent work, point out deficiencies, and suggest ways to improve. Like speed reading, there is so much to cover that we must learn to *manage on the run.*

Evaluating on the run, or continuous performance feedback, offers a number of attractions:

- Only once a year (December or on the anniversary of the employee's hiring) is appraisal directly linked to salary. All other reviews can focus freely on developing more efficient and effective job skills.
- Feedback, positive and negative, follows on the performance, making it possible to take immediate corrective action.
- Appraisals are more likely to be based on a larger sample of work behavior than if restricted to events occurring just prior to the annual interview.
- Frequent dialogue minimizes misunderstandings and surprises ("You never told me that!") between managers and employees.

PRD is designed to improve performance, not dictate compensation.

PRD demands year-round evaluation, not once-a-year rituals.

Promoting productivity through appraisal requires managers to:

- Be genuinely interested in subordinates and their jobs or careers.
- Spend time and energy in defining realistic goals.
- Plan and carry out regular review sessions, insuring that employees know what is expected and how they are performing.

- Expect high performance from themselves and their subordinates.
- Take time to objectively evaluate employee strengths and weaknesses, and consider employee reactions to the evaluation process.
- Learn from each appraisal, and build on mistakes as well as on successes.

Whatever this book can do in making suggestions or codifying processes is overshadowed by the appraiser's enthusiasm and commitment. Half-hearted, *proforma* applications will be of little consequence. Especially important is managerial resolve to know employees and to sustain those wholesome interactions that lead to upgraded work performance.

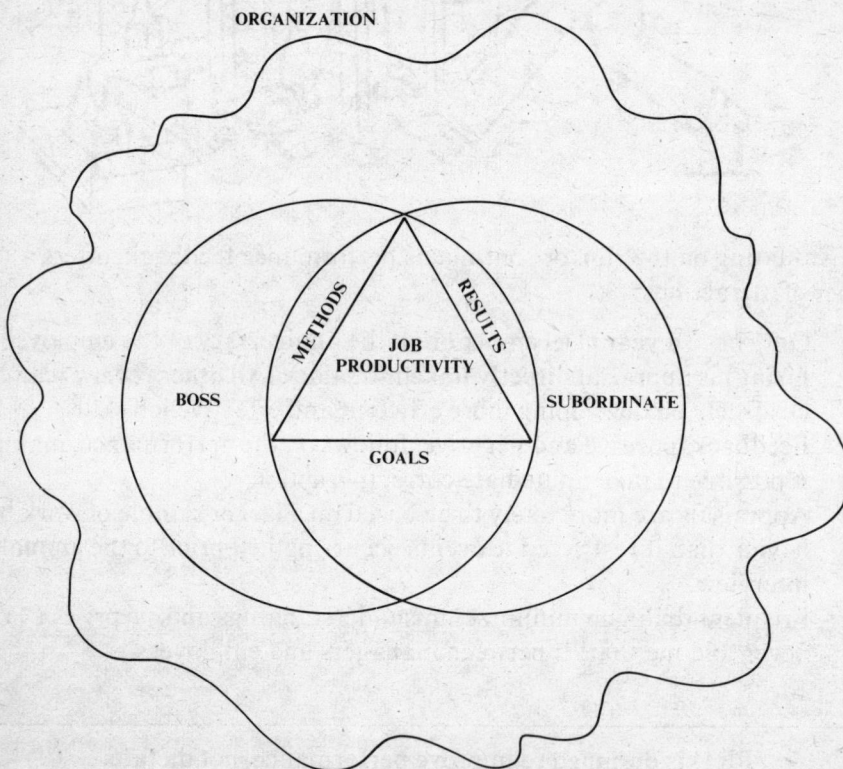

Elements Involved in an Evaluation

Bosses and subordinates operate within the organizational environment and precedents, interacting around a common experience: the job. Goals are jointly established; methods are identified (and invented) to achieve those goals. The outcomes or results are measured against the original goals. Sometimes methods are evaluated to insure that the job is performed within preset budgets and standards of quality.

Goals and methodology are set within the constraints and freedoms of the organization. To a large degree, the success of evaluative processes depends on the ability of bosses and subordinates to establish common experiences (overlapping circles). Out of these, procedures and targets emerge, along with a means to measure their productiveness.

Performance Review and Development can be derived from the general scheme diagrammed on the previous page. The diagram below outlines the six elements of PRD (drawn from Chapter 12 in the author's *Managing the Interview,* published by John Wiley & Sons, Inc., 1980).

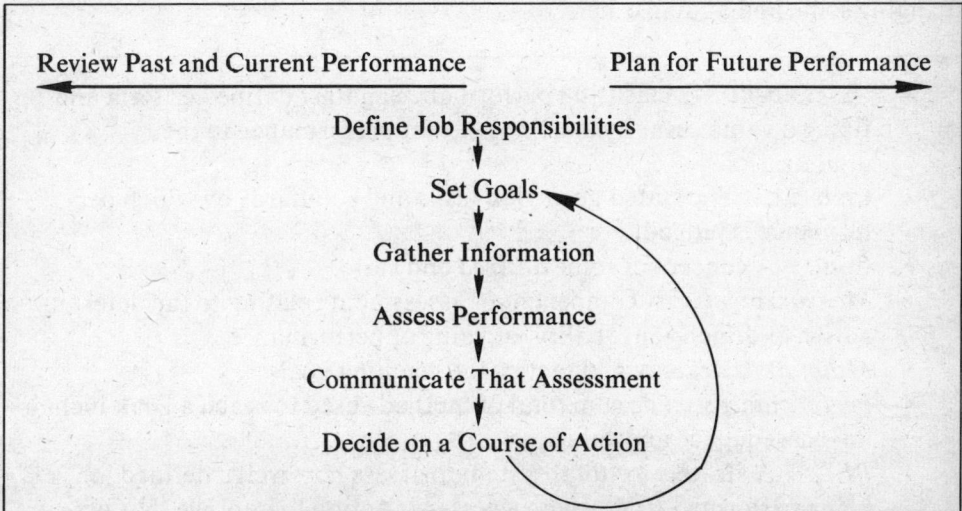

Review Past and Current Performance ← → Plan for Future Performance

Define Job Responsibilities

Set Goals

Gather Information

Assess Performance

Communicate That Assessment

Decide on a Course of Action

Performance Review and Development

As they review and plan, managers must define job responsibilities and specific goals relating to those responsibilities, gather periodic information on performance toward set goals, assess that performance, communicate the assessment to subordinates, and decide on a course of action (set new goals) to develop and expand employee productiveness.

PRD cannot be "just another Personnel program." It must become an integral part of the managing process in order to systematically eliminate bias and uninformed judgments, and to begin to establish a modest, standardized base of information for decision-making and management control.

PRD responds both to the problems discussed in Chapter 1 and the needs presented in Chapter 2. It represents a composite system, incorporating the best of the existing appraisal programs. A summary of its features includes:

— A focus on future performance
— Job definition
— Goal orientation
— Manager-employee mutual action
— Systematic ways of gathering and communicating information throughout the year

— Flexibility so that managers can adapt it to their specific functions
— A "do-it-now" orientation
— A uniform procedure

Competence and consistency in treatment, implementation, adherence to standards, involvement of employees, and follow-through determine the maximum value of PRD to the organization. (Note: Although I use PRD throughout the book, you, of course, need to think in terms of your specific appraisal system. As a model, PRD can be a mirror to reflect your practices, while changing some and adding others.)

- *Assessment:* Measuring performance against defined criteria and fixing a value (usually a rating) of that performance to the organization.
- *Criteria:* The stated goals, job tasks and standards by which performance is judged.
- *Goal:* A concept of some *desired* end state.
- *Measurement:* A component of assessment relating to the determination of dimension, quality, or value of performance.
- *Method:* Strategy and tactics for reaching goals.
- *Performance:* The sum total of methods used to reach a goal, including consequence and value.
- *PRD:* A strategy or total system to assess how well a defined job is being performed, and, when necessary , acting to improve that performance. Commonly referred to as *appraisal*.
- *Rating:* The value of an employee's performance as classified on a continuum of grades or rank; positioning the employee on a defined scale.
- *Responsibility:* A definition of work to be done and its assignment.
- *Results:* Descriptions of *actual* end states or goals; the final effects of strategy; a sum of performance.
- *Task:* Any activity or set of activities carried out by employees to attain goals and satisfy responsibilities. Some tasks are directed and some delegated.

Definitions Relating to PRD

Stop for a moment and think about your own corporation. Check (✔) the degree to which the phrases in the form describe your employees.

	Never	Sometimes	Usually	Almost Always
Enjoy work				
Seem committed to the organization				
Waste time				
Hard working				
Handle pressure				
Competent				
Expect you to initiate and solve problems				
Ask questions				
Come up with alternative approaches and solutions				
Know the job				
Resist change				
Do things without being told				
Complain about overwork and difficulty of the job				
Seem interested in or care about the job				

Now let's take a look at what your check marks mean. You will see that numerical values are assigned to each response. Total the numbers that appear in the answer cells you checked.

	Never	Sometimes	Usually	Almost Always
Enjoy work	0	1	2	3
Seem committed to the organization	0	1	2	3
Waste time	3	2	1	0
Hard working	0	1	2	3
Handle pressure	0	1	2	3
Competent	0	1	2	3
Expect you to initiate and solve problems	3	2	1	0
Ask questions	0	1	2	3
Come up with alternative approaches and solutions	0	1	2	3
Know the job	0	1	2	3
Resist change	3	2	1	0
Do things without being told	0	1	2	3
Complain about overwork and difficulty of the job	3	2	1	0
Seem interested in or care about the job	0	1	2	3

Total Score _____

If you scored above 40 on the test, you can throw away this book. Your organization has few problems with employees. They are competent and totally self-motivated. However, if your score was closer to 20, there is a need for an appraisal system that addresses these problems.

No pretense is made that this is a super scientific instrument, but it is a quick way to profile your perception of those who work with you. How many times do you hear, "Today's workers ain't what they used to be; they don't put out much; they're not loyal to the company; they expect others to wait on them; they don't initiate; they don't accept responsibility, and you have to check up on them all the time!" Whether or not these laments are true, they must be confronted during the appraisal process.

Three critical phases in a person's life shape attitudes and work habits:

- Childhood experiences
- Church and schooling
- The job

Organizations have little control over the first two. Therefore, it's incumbent on managers to provide work experiences that promote self-esteem and commitment to development, and appraisal practices that translate such development into improved procedures and production.

The effectiveness of PRD depends, in part, on your conviction that employees *want to participate* in affairs that affect them, and that, given an opportunity and support, they *will initiate* steps to improve themselves.

The paradox of PRD is that, in the process of gaining control over production, a kind of *decontrol* occurs. Employees begin to shoulder more responsibility for their own development and output. As they do so, it becomes the manager's task to support them with resources and patience, a challenge addressed in detail later.

Section two discusses steps and techniques to use in evaluating performance, employing PRD and an MPI (Metropolitan Products, Inc.) appraisal form as working examples.

APPLICATION AND REVIEW

1. Identify 5 objectives of appraisals.

    (a)

    (b)

    (c)

    (d)

    (e)

2. What are the 6 elements of PRD?

    (a)

    (b)

    (c)

    (d)

    (e)

    (f)

3. Check ($\checkmark$) the ones missing in your system. If any, how can you incorporate them into your method of assessing?

4. Appraisal continuity refers to

5. What are two things you can do to shift the emphasis in your appraisals from compensation to development?

    (a)

    (b)

6. Distinguish between the following terms:

    (a) Goal—

    (b) Method—

    (c) Results—

    (d) Assessment—

    (e) Rating—

    (f) PRD—

SUGGESTED RESPONSES

1. Clarify job requirements, assess performance, improve performance, produce information on needs, and achieve greater use of manpower.

2. Define the job, set goals, gather information, assess, communicate, and take action.

4. Gathering data, communicating about performance, and assessing progress on a week-to-week and month-to-month schedule.

5. (a) Conduct appraisal sessions at times when salary is not a consideration.
    (b) Encourage employees to set personal goals and invent new ways to do the job.
    (c) Etc. (ideas that relate to your specific situation)

6. See definitions on page 36.

SECTION TWO

DOING THE APPRAISAL

This section covers techniques, the "nitty gritty" of defining job responsibilities, developing goals, recording data, and assessing performance. Metropolitan Products Inc. (MPI), a fictional company, is introduced as a vehicle for describing PRD in action.

Chapter 4 presents several appraisal formats with criteria for judging them. The MPI form is introduced, with steps for completing it, as one model for analysis.

Chapter 5 delineates a "goal planning" process. The following subjects are included:

— How to define job responsibilities
— Framing goals
— Eight guidelines for setting goals
— Seven guidelines for reviewing goals
— Criteria for judging the appropriateness of a goal.

Chapter 6 develops the necessity for documenting performance, expands on EEO implications, establishes criteria for judging the quality of data, emphasizes the need to say much in a few words, and suggests ways to gather relevant information to insure fair decisions.

The final chapter in this section distinguishes between appraisal, assessment, and the rating. Topics expanded on are:

— The relationship between ratings and employee development
— The complexities of rating job performance
— Bias in ratings
— Procedures for determining a rating.

CHAPTER 4

THE APPRAISAL FORM

"I won't sign that form, it's
   not fair."

"What's this human relations stuff?
   Can you define it?"

"That form is no different from some
   of those rinky-dink tests we had
   in college."

"How come I didn't get a copy of that?"

Forms can cause more problems than they alleviate, as the four quotations attest. Though some records may seem unnecessary, documentation is an accepted fact of life in the business world. It's important to establish ground rules for good paperwork. This chapter presents a model form for discussion and comparison, but first, let's examine a non-model.

The year before President Jimmy Carter was defeated for election by Ronald Reagan, he decided to evaluate all of his staff as part of a house-cleaning effort. The form he used is reproduced on the next page, with a journalist's tongue-in-cheek-appraisal of the then Chief Executive. It illustrates that even forms and procedures at the highest level in government need revamping and upgrading. From it, we can gain some perspective and humor.

Even though most of the questions employ a six-point scale (No. 8 uses seven points and No. 22 uses percentages), the form is highly subjective. For instance, what is meant by:

— conceptionalize?	— stable?
— controlling quality?	— bright?
— confidence?	— range of information?
— self-doubting?	— smooth?
— judgment?	— charming?
— mature?	— aggressive?
— flexible?	— hostile?
— politically skilled?	

Nation

If Jimmy Took Ham's Test

A remarkable form designed to assess the strengths and weaknesses of high Administration officials was distributed last week by new Chief of Staff Hamilton Jordan. It was devised by Michael Berman, staff counsel and deputy chief of staff to Vice President Walter Mondale, and Len Hirsch, an outside consultant to Jordan. Several management experts who studied the form declared that it told more about the raters than it did about the rated. They viewed it variously as "unsophisticated," "unprofessional," "unfair" and "unreliable." The hastily devised form even included two spelling errors, "savy" and "uncomforable." Here is a specimen on which Washington Bureau Chief Robert Ajemian has evaluated the country's most important employee.

STAFF EVALUATION

Please answer each of the following questions about this person.

Office: *TIME Washington Bureau*
Name of Rater: *Robert Ajemian, Bureau Chief*

Name: *Jimmy Carter*
Salary: *$200,000*
Position: *President of the U.S.*

Duties: *Governing the nation as chief of the Executive Branch, Commander in Chief of the armed forces, head of the Democratic Party*

Work Habits

1) On the average when does this person:
   arrive at work *before anybody else*
   leave work *before anybody else*

2) Pace of Work:
   1 2 3 4 5 (6)
   slow   fast

3) Level of Effort:
   1 2 3 4 5 (6)
   below   full
   capacity   capacity

4) Quality of Work:
   1 2 (3) 4 5 6
   poor   good

5) What is he/she best at? (rank 1-5)
   _3_ Conceptualizing
   _2_ Planning
   _5_ Implementing
   _1_ Attending to detail
   _4_ Controlling quality

6) Does this person have the skills to do the job he/she was hired to do?
   yes ___
   no ___
   ? *not yet*

7) Would the slot filled by this person be better filled by someone else?
   yes ___
   no ___
   ? *not yet*

Personal Characteristics:

8) How confident is this person? (circle one)
   x   x   x   x   (x)   x
   self   confident   cocky
   doubting

9) How confident are you of this person's judgment?
   1 2 (3) 4 5 6
   not   very
   confident   confident

10) How mature is this person?
    1 2 3 4 5 (6)
    immature   mature

11) How flexible is this person?
    1 (2) 3 4 5 6
    rigid   flexible

12) How stable is this person?
    1 2 3 4 5 (6)
    erratic   steady

13) How frequently does this person come up with new ideas?
    1 (2) 3 4 5 6
    seldom   often

14) How open is this person to new ideas?
    1 2 3 4 5 (6)
    closed   open

15) How bright is this person?
    1 2 3 4 (5) 6
    average   very bright

16) What are this person's special talents?
    1) *tenacious belief in self*
    2) *antagonizing Congress*
    3) *can work with White House staff*

17) What is this person's range of information?
    1 2 3 4 (5) 6
    narrow   broad

Interpersonal Relations:

18) How would you characterize this person's impact on other people? (for example, hostile, smooth, aggressive, charming, etc)
    1) *tranquillizing*
    2) *believable*
    3) *makes people think of Edward Kennedy*

19) How well does this person get along with
    Superiors   1 2 3 4 5 (6)
    Peers   1 2 3 4 5 (6)
    Subordinates (1) 2 3 4 5 6
    Outsiders   (1) 2 3 4 5 6
                 not well   very well

20) In a public setting, how comfortable would you be having this person represent:
    you or your office 1 2 3 4 5 (6)
    The President   1 2 (3) 4 5 6
                   uncomforable   comfortable

21) Rate this person's political skills.
    1 (2) 3 4 5 6
    naive   savy

Supervision and Direction

22) To what extent is this person focused on accomplishing the
    Administration's goals *40%*
    personal goals   *60%*
                            _____
                            100 %

23) How capable is this person at working toward implementing a decision with which he/she may not agree?
    (1) 2 3 4 5 6
    reluctant   eager

24) How well does this person take direction?
    (1) 2 3 4 5 6
    resists   readily

25) How much supervision does this person need?
    1 2 (3) 4 5 6
    a lot   little

26) How readily does this person offer to help out by doing that which is not a part of his/her "job"?
    1 2 3 4 5 (6)
    seldom   often

Summary:

27) Can this person assume more responsibility?
    yes ___
    no ___
    ? *already has too much*

28) List this person's 3 major strengths and 3 major weaknesses.
    Strengths: 1) *high sense of decency and moral values*
    2) *identifies problems well*
    3) *rarely flaps*
    Weaknesses: 1) *dislikes admitting mistakes*
    2) *substitutes pieties for programs*
    3) *inability to cut loose from subordinates*

29) List this person's 3 major accomplishments.
    1) *brought balanced approach to Middle East*
    2) *aligned America more with forces of change in the world*
    3) *visiting average Americans in their homes*

30) List 3 things about this person that have disappointed you.
    1) *has no clear public philosophy*
    2) *attracted too little excellence to Government*
    3) *doesn't use power with confidence*

Also, what behaviors distinguish a "5" performance from a "4" or "3"? The *Summary* is the best part of the form. Most of the other questions rely on the "gut feelings" of the boss. Ratings would not likely be duplicated if used by different raters.

In Chapter 1, you were asked to note the criteria you use in appraisals. Divide them according to the taxonomy of criteria detailed below. To gain maximum value from this chapter, I suggest you periodically refer to one of *your* completed appraisals for comparison.

The items on an appraisal form can usually be divided into four types:

- Traits
- Tasks
- Goals
- Job Behaviors

The *TRAIT* approach has been around for a long time. The form lists personal qualities for managers to rate, such as initiative, effort, dependability, leadership, analytical ability, judgment, creativity, attitude, maturity, critical thinking, enthusiasm, versatility, self-control, thoroughness, accuracy, sincerity. These seem logical and are easy to embrace, but assessing them poses two serious EEO considerations:

- Do raters agree on the definition for each characteristic?
- Are the traits job related?

The *Personal Characteristics* section of the Jimmy Carter appraisal illustrates this potential problem.

The *TASK* approach (see form below) usually presents a list of typical functions — planning, organizing, producing, knowing the job, delegating, handling people, meeting deadlines, following through, and so on.

1. Plans—anticipates needs, sets priorities, schedules steps to achieve goals.

Unsatisfactory	Marginal	Acceptable	Exceptional	Outstanding

2. Organizes—the division of labor, time schedule, materials and equipment to obtain efficient and effective results.

Unsatisfactory	Marginal	Acceptable	Exceptional	Outstanding

Task Form

An increasingly popular method is based on *GOALS* (the results desired in a job). A goal form contains a section for setting goals and one for reviewing progress. Goals have the potential to be job specific, as shown in the Goal Form. The next chapter elaborates on goal setting.

Goals	Weight	How Measured	Deadline	Achieved	Not Achieved	Undetermined
1. Achieve $7½ million in annual sales.	60%	By direct orders received	Mar. 30-30% Jun. 30-20% Sep. 30-20% Dec. 31-30%			
2. Improve knowledge of competitors	10%	By ability to respond to questions in sales presentations	March			

Goal Form

1. What is your assessment of the employee's performance on the technical aspects of the job? (Be specific.)

_____

_____

_____

_____

2. What is your evaluation of the employee's ability to manage others? (Be specific.)

_____

_____

_____

_____

Job Behavior Descriptive Form

JOB BEHAVIOR criteria can take two forms: 1) open ended, essay-type descriptions and 2) predetermined job behaviors. In the former, a description of an employee's performance is written out with work examples (see form on page 48).

In the latter, the critera are preset, based on a job analysis (see below).

| Never | Seldom | Sometimes | Usually | Always |

```
|_____|_____|_____|_____|
1        2        3        4        5
```

Using the above scale, write the appropriate rating to the left of each item, indicating to what extent the employee exhibited that behavior.

— Writes clear, easily understood reports.
— Completes projects on time.
— Is open to subordinates' ideas.
— Is well-liked by team members.
— Shows patience when training new employees.
— Gives credit to subordinates for good work.
— Contributes new approaches to old problems.

Job Behavior Form

Of course, a form may consist of a combination of the four types of criteria, e.g., traits and tasks, tasks and job behaviors, goals and job behavior. Whatever appraisal form is used, it should provide an opportunity to adequately describe an employee's performance and meet EEO standards.

Below, list what you consider the ingredients of an effective appraisal form. Note length, content, format, rating system, etc.

Using the features you consider important, plus the six measures that follow, judge the utility of your form and the model in this chapter.

An appraisal form should be matched against the following standards:

Simplicity — Is it easy to understand? Easy to administer? Does it require an inordinate amount of time to complete? No organization needs to add to its pile of paperwork. An appraisal form should be clean, clear and concise.

Relevancy — Does the form require information related directly to the tasks and responsibilities of the job, and does it reflect the sequence a manager is expected to follow in appraising performance?

Descriptiveness — Does the form require managers to cite examples of the employee's performance, both good and bad? If done well, and the ratings are clearly defined, an "outsider" ought to be able to read a completed form and arrive at the same rating as the appraiser.

Adaptability — Does the form allow managers in different functions and departments to adapt it to their particular needs and situations? Appraising a sales representative is not the same as appraising an engineer, a foreman, or a marketing researcher. The form should encourage flexible usage.

Comprehensiveness — Does the form allow space to describe the total job for the total time period? Abbreviated formats invite managers to record only recent events and dominant behaviors of the employee.

Objectivity — Are criteria defined so all rates assess the same factors? Does the form encourage consistency? Is it scaled to the EEO yardstick?

For purposes of walking through and filling out an appraisal form, reproduce the PRD form from the mythical company, MPI. MPI is not any one company: it is everyone's organization. To give it life, a brief vita is supplied. MPI demonstrates one way to appraise performance.

SECTION A PERFORMANCE REVIEW & DEVELOPMENT

INSTRUCTIONS: Define job responsibilities, review goals, (Goal Planning Insert), add relevant tasks; then rate them and give specific examples of performance to support your assessment. **Be specific. Complete all sections.**

Name	Job Title	Date

SECTION A.
JOB RESPONSIBILITIES/GOALS

Briefly list the major responsibilities for this position. Weight each responsibility according to its importance. For each responsibility, note specific goals set with the employee (on the Goal Planning Insert).

JOB RESPONSIBILITIES
Rate the employee on each responsibility, and give examples of the employee's performance (or lack of) that most accurately describe your rating.

	Weight	OUTSTANDING	COMPETENT	MARGINAL
(1)	%			
Examples:				
(2)	%			
Examples:				
(3)	%			
Examples:				
(4)	%			
Examples:				
(5)	%			
Examples:				

SECTION B. PERFORMANCE TASKS

Listed below and on the facing page are four categories of tasks that relate to job performance. Under each category, list additional ones specific to this job position. Rate the employee on each applicable factor. If a printed task does not apply, skip it and go on to the next one. Cite specific examples of employee performance and/or lack of performance.

KNOWS THE JOB	OUTSTANDING	COMPETENT	MARGINAL
Demonstrates knowledge of job requirements, skills, procedures, techniques and principles.			
Keeps current on changes in technical knowledge.			
Expands knowledge of the job and how it relates to other jobs.			
Other:			
Examples of "KNOWS THE JOB" that describe your ratings:			

RELATES TO PEOPLE ON THE JOB	OUTSTANDING	COMPETENT	MARGINAL
Develops subordinates.			
Acts as part of a team.			
Practices 2-way communications.			
Motivates subordinates to accomplish their goals.			
Leads by example.			
Other:			
Examples of "RELATES TO PEOPLE ON THE JOB" that describe your ratings:			

MANAGES THE JOB	OUTSTANDING	COMPETENT	MARGINAL
Recognizes problems.			
Analyzes causes of problems.			
Generates alternative approaches.			
Sets realistic goals.			
Establishes work priorities.			
Organizes people and materials to reach goals.			
Handles pressure.			
Evaluates results.			
Operates within Affirmative Action Plans.			
Other:			

Examples of "MANAGES THE JOB" that describe your ratings:

GETS THE JOB DONE	OUTSTANDING	COMPETENT	MARGINAL
Initiates solutions.			
Follows through.			
Meets deadlines.			
Achieves balance between work quality and quantity.			
Takes responsibility for actions.			
Other:			

Examples of "GETS THE JOB DONE" that describe your ratings:

SECTION C. SUMMARY

Name of Employee		Position
Unit		Location
Years with Company	Years in Present Position	Years Under Your Supervision

COMMENTS ON STRENGTHS AND ACCOMPLISHMENTS

Identify the two or three most significant strengths and job accomplishments.

(1)

(2)

(3)

COMMENTS ON AREAS REQUIRING DEVELOPMENT

Identify two or three areas where this employee needs to improve. (Set new goals).

(1)

(2)

(3)

PERFORMANCE ASSESSMENT

OVERALL RATING (check one)

OUTSTANDING ☐   COMPETENT ☐   MARGINAL ☐

Previous Rating	Previous Rating By	Date of Previous Rating

If there is a change in rating, state the major reason for that change.

EMPLOYEE COMMENTS (Use additional paper, if necessary)

PERFORMANCE REVIEW AND COMMUNICATION

Prepared By	Date	Reviewed With Employee	Date

METROPOLITAN PRODUCTS INC. VITA

MPI is a Fortune 500, internationally known conglomerate. It has six major divisions:

- Construction Equipment
- Automotive Parts
- Packaging—containers, bottles, cartons
- Chemicals—fertilizers
- Health and Beauty Products
- Pharmaceuticals

In addition, MPI has a large international operation with four central offices in Europe, Africa, Asia and South America.

The corporate headquarters is in Riverton.

MPI has an aggressive program of acquisitions, which has led to its six major divisions.

Last year's sales were $800 million, with projections of over $1 billion this year. MPI has enjoyed 25 years of consecutive growth. Its stock is currently selling for 65½ with an annual dividend of $2.10.

MPI is noted for its sound marketing/sales strategies and actions.

MPI employees total 23,000 worldwide.

The growth rate has made it imperative that MPI begin an aggressive program for developing managers at all levels. This year, they are installing a performance appraisal system called Performance Review and Development (PRD).

Attempting to comply with the six criteria of simplicity, relevancy, descriptiveness, adaptability, comprehensiveness and objectivity, the MPI form balances essay and checklist, specific goals and predetermined tasks, and simplicity with comprehensiveness. Treat it as an example, not as the model: there is no *one* correct format. A well-constructed form can help, but it is no substitute for the skilled hands that complete it.

STEPS IN COMPLETING THE PRD FORM

The following steps outline a procedure for filling out the appraisal form.

1. Spell out the major responsibilities of the job (Section A). Chapter 5 details this process.
2. Review and judge the extent to which preset goals for each responsibility have been accomplished, (MPI provides an addendum Goal Planning Insert—also covered in the next chapter.)
3. Rate the employee's performance on each responsibility. In MPI, the three ratings are:

Outstanding: Performance consistently exceeds all requirements associated with the job. Unique, exceptional accomplishments are clearly obvious to all. The employee consistently demonstrates the highest level of work that has a significant and positive impact toward attaining departmental and overall organizational goals. This person is top notch, one of our stars.

Competent: Performance meets the requirements associated with the job. Accomplishments are clearly in accord with job demands. This person usually performs satisfactorily, and sometimes commendably, achieving the full scope of the assigned position. There are areas in which the employee can improve, but overall he/she consistently and capably meets normal expectations. Though some employees may sort out as high competent and some as low, generally most employees will fall within this *competent* range.

Marginal: Performance does not meet most standards associated with the job. Accomplishments are below job demands. This person obviously needs improvement. If, after remedial measures (e.g. training), performance continues at an unacceptable level, the employee should be reassigned or terminated.

4. Complete Section B of the PRD form:
   — Add tasks specific to the position being assessed.
   — Rate the employee on all *applicable* tasks.
   — Cite examples of performance to support the ratings.
Since most appraisals include performance tasks, they are discussed in detail later in this chapter.
5. List the major accomplishments of the employee (Section C).
6. Identify two or three areas of performance that need to be improved. (The last section of this book is devoted to the specifics of converting appraisals into employee development.)
7. Weighing the sub-ratings and word descriptions of achievement, rate the employee on overall performance and cite reasons for a change, if any, from the previous rating.

PERFORMANCE TASKS

Tasks like the ones inventoried in *Section B* of the PRD form represent processes that are the means and ends to accomplishing specific goals. They slice a different view of assessment, a second look that can be dovetailed with goals. Employees at all levels must demonstrate a modest knowledge of the job, relate effectively with people, manage the work, and, of course, accomplish the job.

Adaptability was one measure of an effective appraisal form. Managers ought to add and delete data, fitting the form to their function. The next few pages give examples of how to turn tasks into behaviors that are specific to a particular job.

Knows the Job refers to a clear understanding of the skills and processes necessary to perform the job. The knowledge may be standard (using a dictionary) or highly technical (understanding the principles of hydraulics).

The job may require knowledge about a lot of things (V-P of operations), or a lot of knowledge about a few things (corporate tax lawyer). The total knowledge of a particular job is a combination of scope and depth.

To supplement the three *knowledge* tasks on the PRD form, add some of your own under the heading "Other" below.

KNOWS THE JOB	OUTSTANDING	COMPETENT	MARGINAL
Demonstrates knowledge of job requirements, skills, procedures, techniques and principles.			
Keeps current on changes in technical knowledge.			
Expands knowledge of the job and how it relates to other jobs.			
Other:			
Examples of "KNOWS THE JOB" that describe your ratings:			

PRD Form

Here are some tasks tailored to specific job titles:

—	District Sales Manager	Is aware of market conditions, trends and competitor activity.
—	Sales Representative	Keeps current on competitor products and strategies.
—	Product Manager	Has working knowledge of the fundamentals of advertising (creative and media) and sales promotion.
—	Manager, Cost Accounting	Is up-to-date on usury law and legal documents.
—	Plant Accountant	Knows and understands material usage variances.
—	Design Engineer	Keeps current through contact with customer and field reps. about quality problems.
—	Plant Manager	Is knowledgeable about latest safety procedures.
—	Shift Supervisor	Knows the key terms of the union contract.

Some examples that show the level of knowledge include:

—	District Sales Manager	Gave thorough presentation on competing products at the National Sales Assembly.
—	Sales Representative	Demonstrated complete knowledge of our "Big D" deodorant in direct account presentations.
—	Product Manager	Demonstrated command of the job by teaching assistant product managers procedures and general business practices.

— Plant Accountant	Understood the details of accounting but not of manufacturing systems.
— Design Engineer	Demonstrated a working knowledge of the hoist cylinder component.
— Plant Manager	Did not demonstrate a working knowledge of the Affirmative Action Plan.
— Shift Supervisor	Showed good grasp of OSHA regulations—identified three potential safety violations in the plant.

Which of the above examples gives you the best picture of the employee's work?

The worst picture?

The most descriptive examples apply to the district sales manager, the sales representative, the product manager, and the supervisor. The most general and least measurable samples of performance are cited for the: Plant Accountant — the employee would likely respond, "What do you mean? What's the evidence for *not manufacturing systems?*"; the Design Engineer — *How* did the employee demonstrate a working knowledge? and the Plant Manager — What did the manager fail to know or do?

Relates to People includes motivating and getting along with subordinates, colleagues, personnel in other departments, and superiors.

Five tasks are specified on the PRD form. Write in others that you feel are important.

RELATES TO PEOPLE ON THE JOB	OUTSTANDING	COMPETENT	MARGINAL
Develops subordinates.			
Acts as part of a team.			
Practices two-way communications.			
Motivates subordinates to accomplish their goals.			
Leads by example.			
Other:			

Examples of "RELATES TO PEOPLE ON THE JOB"
that describe your ratings:

PRD FORM

Some suggested *Relates to People* tasks are:

— District Sales Manager   Handles sales representatives based on their individual strengths and weaknesses.

— Sales Representative   Maintains a rapport with customers.

— Product Manager   Communicates and negotiates with people outside the department.

— Plant Accountant   Trains junior accountants.

— Shift Supervisor   Maintains a harmonious relationship with workers and union representatives.

Some examples of *Relates to People* performance include:

— District Sales Manager	Helped one rep. develop a better working relationship with the *Shop and Save* account.
— Sales Representative	Distributors say the individual is well-liked.
— Manager, Cost Accounting	Visited each plant manager at least once a quarter.
— Plant Accountant	Established monthly meetings for subordinates to air problems and suggested ways to improve departmental operations.
— Design Engineer	Alienated the plant manager by failing to keep him informed during the new hoist test.
— Filling Department Head	Two supervisors recently promoted after working and training under him.
— Shift Supervisor	Reassigned two workers to increase efficiency of materials movement.

Manages the Job is the "how," the process, the way one administers job responsibilities. This set of tasks encompasses the traditional management functions of planning, controlling, deciding, analyzing, and evaluating.

To stimulate thinking in this area, eight activities appear on the PRD form. Add any additional ones that you find pertinent.

MANAGES THE JOB	OUTSTANDING	COMPETENT	MARGINAL
Recognizes problems.			
Analyzes causes of problems.			
Generates alternative approaches.			
Sets realistic goals.			
Establishes work priorities.			
Organizes people and materials to reach goals.			
Handles pressure situations.			
Evaluates results.			
Operates within Affirmative Action Plans.			
Other:			
Examples of "MANAGES THE JOB" that describe your ratings:			

PRD Form

Sample tasks for six job positions are defined below:

— Sales Representative Plans the territory.

— Manager, Cost Accounting Identifies cost-saving procedures for manufacturing.

— Design Engineer Monitors designs through to pilot run.

— Filling Department Head Develops a contingency plan in case of equipment failure.

— Shift Supervisor Keeps accurate records.

— Product Manager Utilizes the resources of support groups.

For specific examples that portray the employee *managing the job*, consider the following:

— District Sales Manager	Determined why sales were down 40 percent in the *K-Mart* account.
— Sales Representative	Planned her time to see all accounts monthly.
— Plant Accountant	Did not control overtime in Accounts Payable Department.
— Filling Department Head	Reorganized production when main belt was out for two days.
— Shift Supervisor	Did not allocate work effectively — many worker complaints.

Gets the Job Done is the measured effect of performance on end results. How answerable for actions and consequences is the employee? Was each of the major goals met?

Again to start your thinking, consider the five tasks decribed on PRD form below, then add others you think of.

GETS THE JOB DONE	OUTSTANDING	COMPETENT	MARGINAL
Initiates solutions.			
Follows through.			
Meets deadlines.			
Achieves balance between work quality and quantity.			
Takes responsibility for actions.			
Other:			
Examples of "GETS THE JOB DONE" that describe your ratings:			

PRD Form

Other tasks might include:

— District Sales Manager	Meets quarterly sales quotas.
— Sales Representative	Maintains customer call average.
— Manager, Cost Accounting	Develops improvement programs (e.g., cost recording, cost reduction).
— Plant Accountant	Submits accurate, on time, monthly manufacturing reports.
— Design Engineer	Redesigns hoist assemblies.
— Filling Department Head	Meets emergency production deadlines.
— Shift Supervisor	Maintains low level of absenteeism.

Examples of *Gets the Job Done* performance would be:

— District Sales Manager	Achieved 110 percent of the budget for the district with proper product line distribution.
— Sales Representative	Did not maintain eight calls per day and was behind schedule in calling on 25 percent of her key accounts.
— Manager, Cost Accounting	Did not meet four of the monthly closings.
— Plant Accountant	Completed the internal control questionnaire before due date.
— Design Engineer	Did not follow through with implementing the hoist cylinder design.

— Shift Supervisor   Achieved 25 percent drop
in absenteeism.

By design, this chapter has been a series of examples and illustrations. Form filling is not appraising, but it records the assessment for all to see. With criteria such as tasks, or whatever type of form, you must give as complete a picture as possible. Be specific, recount critical job incidents, and document. PRD is a winnowing sequence, moving from abstract job descriptions to concrete performance.

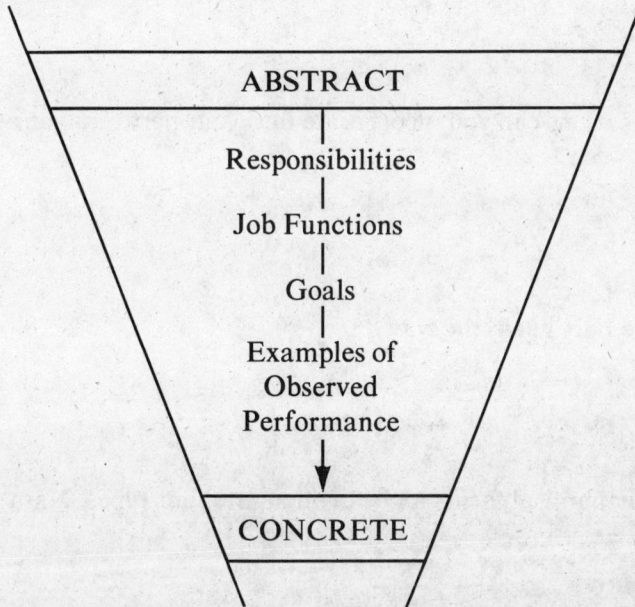

ABSTRACT

Responsibilities

Job Functions

Goals

Examples of
Observed
Performance

CONCRETE

APPLICATION AND REVIEW

1. Compare your form to the MPI form.
   What are the similaritities?

   What are the differences?

   What applications can you incorporate into your performance appraisal practice?

   What would only get in the way?

2. Items on an appraisal form can be divided into four types. Name them.
   (a)
   (b)
   (c)
   (d)

3. List the criteria for judging the adequacy of a performance appraisal form.
   (a)
   (b)
   (c)
   (d)
   (e)
   (f)
   Does your current form satisfy all six criteria?

4. Based on working with the examples in this chapter, check all traits and tasks on your current appraisal form and define them in specific job terms.

SUGGESTED RESPONSES

1. Your responses will vary.
2. Traits, tasks, goals, job behaviors.
3. Simplicity, relevancy, descriptiveness, adaptability, comprehensiveness, objectivity.
4. Your responses will vary.

CHAPTER 5

RESPONSIBILITIES
AND GOALS

"I didn't know that was part of my job."
"Whose goals? They're sure not mine."
"You never told me about that."
"All this goal setting stuff is a lot of Mickey Mouse."

You may have been on the sending or receiving end of one of the above confrontations. Confusion in PRD (Performance Review and Development) can almost always be traced to inadequate procedures for defining job responsibilities and setting goals.

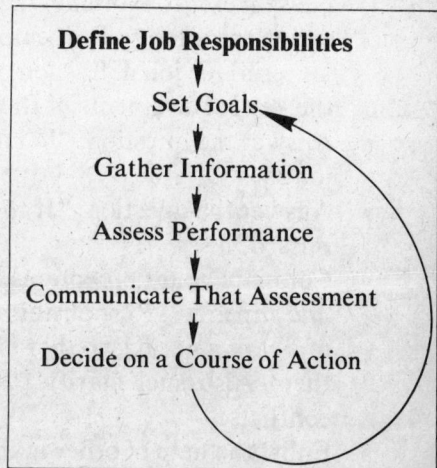

Define Job Responsibilities
↓
Set Goals
↓
Gather Information
↓
Assess Performance
↓
Communicate That Assessment
↓
Decide on a Course of Action

DEFINING
JOB
RESPONSIBILITIES

A major danger with job descriptions is ambiguity. Written definitions do not guarantee understanding. Repetition and feedback are necessary.

Test this by trying the following experiment. Identify a job position you supervise. List the five major responsibilities of that job in order of importance, from most critical to least critical.

Job position _____

Job Responsibilities (rank in order of importance)

1.

2.

3.

4.

5.

Seal your response in an envelope; then ask a subordinate to do the same. Simultaneously open the envelopes and compare the results, noting the similarities and differences. I predict that you will find at least one job responsibility on each list that is not on the other, and one or more major discrepancies in the rank ordering of responsibilities.

Chapter 1 stressed that performance reviews are biased by likes and dislikes, current events, politics, promotability, central tendency, traditions and an infinity of variables. One way to avoid such traps and to become more objective is to clarify the requirements of the job, the first step in any appraisal.

How do you arrive at job responsibilities?

- Analyze the job description, if one exists. If it is inadequate and out of phase (refer to Notion 4 in Chater 1), rewrite it. Make position descriptions into *living* documents. They can provide useful reference material for job definition, which is simply a realistic explanation of the key requirements of the job.
- Answer the question: "What does it take to successfully perform the job?"
- Answer the question: "If the job were eliminated, what would be missed?"
- Compare your perceptions of the job with those of your subordinates *and* superiors. Responsibilities should bc delineated at the beginning of a rating period, so that employees understand what is expected of them. Also, such clarification with superiors can prevent potential conflicts.
- Enlist the help of other managers who supervise the same job position and reach a consensus on responsibilities.
  For instance, some primary responsibilities for an accountant might be to:
    - Prepare monthly financial reports
    - Prepare a formal analysis for financial statements
    - Analyze and research unusual changes in operating expenses.

Examples of responsibilities for other positions are noted below:

— Sales Representative   Market and sell company products through assigned distributors.

Meet or exceed the territory sales budget.

— Manager, Cost Accounting	Coordinate the annual physical inventory.
— Programmer Analyst	Analyze, design, develop and implement EDP systems of limited complexity.
— Design Engineer	Lay out components or systems within given guidelines and design criteria.
— Plant Manager	Plan, forecast and control imprint production costs within financial objectives for relevant sales volume and product mix.
— Shift Supervisor	Control scrap and reoperation.
	Maintain standard shift output with standard line manning.

Identifying responsibilities is a deceptively complex task. *Copying job descriptions will not suffice!* Responsibilities must be phrased so that observable goals can be derived from them. Clearly detailed job requirements, understood by all parties, make it easier to establish and judge the extent to which the employee reaches those goals.

The reliability and validity of your appraisals are in direct proportion to the degree of definition and understanding about what the job entails.

Like responsibilities, goals should be spelled out at the beginning of a rating period. In the PRD interview, these preset goals are reviewed. Since clear goals lead to sound appraisals, the rest of this chapter discusses framing goals, setting goals, and reviewing goals.

FRAMING GOALS

Goals express what should be achieved during the evaluation period. Usually a goal is stated as a result, an end state. Goals emphasize the future, where the organization is going. They present a statement of purpose and direction, and form a common starting point for developmental plans.

Goals range from simple (type 40 words per minute), to complicated (discover a new product); from routine (sweep the floors), to emergencies (e.g. equipment breakdowns, production changes, back orders, switches in priorities). In all cases, they must be stated specifically enough so they can be measured.

Consider the goal "needs to develop a better attitude." As stated, it is not measurable. If a poor attitude means that the employee disagrees with every idea suggested by the boss, then the goal could be rephrased to: "Over the next 90 days, this employee will agree with and support 50 percent of the ideas submitted by the boss." An exaggerated example, but, nonetheless, it emphasizes the need to write goals (and the methods to achieve them) in terms that can be observed and evaluated by both boss and subordinate.

Sometimes procedures and methods must be specified along with the results. If a sales rep 's goal is to "achieve $7 million in sales in the calendar year," that is an end result. If the representative is expected to maintain good relationships with distributors, customers, and service personnel, then *the way* he or she goes about achieving sales is also a standard to be met. For example, the rep could burn out the territory to reach the $7 million quota, leaving disgruntled customers and distributors to be contended with during the next year.

> Means *and* ends, methods *and* goals, should be designated and discussed at the beginning of the evaluation period.

Managers frequently tell employees that "results are what count," then grade them on methodology. I know an executive who was hired by the chairman of the board and told to "get this company out of the red." He did, and was fired because he "ruffled too many feathers" in the process. The chairman

Goals	Methods	Results
Simple		
Complex		
Crisis		

Goal Matrix

rated him on pro*cess*, not pro*duct*. Assessing methods is unfair, *unless* managers label them as standards when goals are set.

One way to think about goals and methods is depicted in the Goal Matrix on page 72.

The matrix also indicates that, even though method is defined as the *strategy and tactics for achieving a goal,* method and goals overlap. Ends frequently become means and means, ends. Calling on eight customers per day could be a goal, but it is also a procedure for attaining quotas. And maintaining quarterly quotas is a means of meeting the annual sales goal.

Given these qualifications, the matrix can help by:

- Providing a different way to think about goals.
- Deliberately separating methods from results, reminding managers that both must be stated.
- Emphasizing the need to weight goals—i.e., attaining complex and crisis goals would be a greater achievement than accomplishing simpler ones.

A simple scheme, it can help to illustrate the process and problems of creating goals. Though some fall in between, goals are grouped into two extremes—simple and complex. The third category assumes that, because of the inherent pressure in emergencies, *crisis* goals are distinct. They may be anticipated, but, unlike simple and complex goals, they are unplanned.

In the matrix below, try your hand at composing goals by writing six examples for a job position with which you are familiar.

Job Position _____

GOAL	METHOD	RESULT
Simple	A.	B.
Complex	C.	D.
Crisis	E.	F.

A. Keep the office neat and clean.

Turn off all equipment at the end of each day.

B. Call on eight customers per day.

Complete a one-page summary of your activities each week.

C. Develop a new approach in handling irate customers.

Cut the budget by 20 percent without reducing sales.

D. Increase business by 20 percent over last year.

Reduce absenteeism from 8 to 4 percent.

E. In all accidents, follow the standard emergency procedures.

Know how to trouble-shoot equipment when it breaks down.

F. Meet sales, even if the economy weakens.

Achieve production quota in the face of schedule changes.

Examples of Goals

Some questions to ask in preparing goals:

— Is the goal *clear*? Do you and the employee understand the desired outcome and how it will be measured?
— Is the goal *realistic*? Does it relate to operations and is it attainable?
— Is the goal *consistent*? Is it in keeping with the job? Does it contradict other goals?
— Is the goal *controllable*? Is it within the employee's power? (A severe winter could work against a supervisor trying to reduce absenteeism.)
— Is the goal *challenging*? Does the employee have to stretch and grow in reaching the goal?
— Is the goal *efficacious*? Will it make a difference in production? In the department? If not achieved, will there be a major gap in operations, or will it be imperceptible?

To test the quality of your six goals (page 73), rate them on each criterion.

1 = low degree of
2 = medium degree of
3 = high degree of

Then total the score for each goal.

Goal	Clarity	Realism	Consistency	Control	Challenge	Efficacy	Totals
1.							
2.							
3.							
4.							
5.							
6.							

A highly desirable goal would total 14-18 points. Of course, some will score lower because not all goals can be challenging or earth-shaking. But most should be understandable, attainable, consistent, and within the employee's control. Goals that do not rate 12 or better should be rewritten until they do.

SETTING GOALS

There are many reasons for setting goals. They help us:

- Clarify where we want to go to better understand how to get there.
- Decode expectations for all to see and understand.
- Communicate more often about the job.
- Establish a foundation upon which to build improvement.
- Coordinate activities with other people and departments who influence the job.
- Provide for a more orderly distribution and scheduling of work.
- Emphasize delegating responsibility.
- Conduct more objective evaluations.

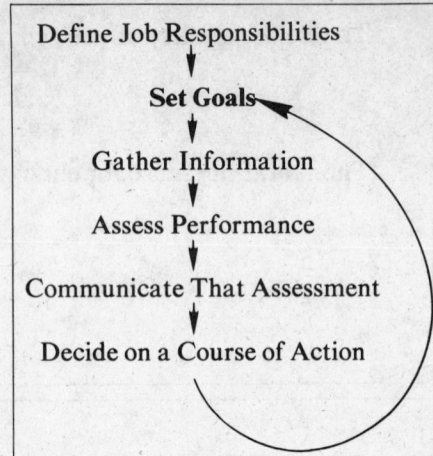

Define Job Responsibilities

↓

Set Goals

↓

Gather Information

↓

Assess Performance

↓

Communicate That Assessment

↓

Decide on a Course of Action

Is there a *best* procedure for setting goals? No, but certain guidelines can help. Eight are outlined below.

1. Ask employees to submit job and personal goals first.
2. Formulate goals for the coming year based on:
   — the organization's goals
   — the operating plan of the division
   — the department or unit goals
   — the particular job to be performed
   — the employee's goals.
3. Communicate the goals to the employee. They should be clear, realistic, consistent, controllable, challenging, and efficacious. Some will be routine and some complex. Some will relate to outcomes and others to methodology.
4. Allow for modification. Ask for the employee's reaction. If necessary, modify and add goals suggested by the employee. Reach agreement on the final goals.

A general guideline: give employees the benefit of the doubt. They and they alone hold the key to goal attainment.

5. Discuss methods to reach the goals. Ask for the employee's input on

ways to attain them. Get the employee's commitment to take action, and briefly outline the necessary steps in writing for each of them to keep as a record.

6. Establish measurement and time lines. For each goal indicate how and when it will be measured. Again allow for the employee's input because assigned deadlines might not be realistic, and there may be additional ways to determine if the goals are being reached.

7. Ask the employee to summarize. When goals are explicitly stated, let the employee enumerate all expectations to insure mutual understanding. Make sure that the employee has a copy of the goals and deadlines.

8. Express confidence and set a review date. Since research suggests that expectations for successful performance govern actual performance, (see the examples of the "G-factor" on page 110) indicate confidence in and support of the employee, and set a reasonable date (60-90 days) to review progress. This date is not meant to be a full-fledged appraisal, but rather a stopping point when manager and employee say, "Hey, how are we doing? Do we need to change anything? Have we left out anything?"

This process is aided in MPI by a *Goal Planning Insert,* shown on succeeding pages. One of the difficult tasks is identifying yardsticks for measuring goals. The psychologist E. L. Thorndike put it this way: "If a thing exists, it exists in some amount. If it exists in some amount, it can be measured." For instance, to measure "improving relationships with another department," consider:

- What behaviors of the employee will indicate improved relations? What behaviors of personnel from the other departments will indicate improved relations?
- What outcomes in the working relationship between the two can be observed?

If measurement cannot be established, the goal should be changed or discarded.

An example of entries on the *Goal Planning Insert* appears on page 80.

MPI GOAL PLANNING INSERT, PART 1

INSTRUCTIONS: Establish goals with the employee that coincide with organizational and departmental goals, the job responsibilities, and the needs of the employee performing the job. Each goal should be numbered. Indicate when it is to be achieved and how it will be measured.

COMPLETE ALL SECTIONS

GOAL SETTING

NAME	JOB TITLE	PERIOD BEGINNING	
Number (Rank in order of importance)	GOAL SETTING	HOW MEASURED (INDICATORS)	WHEN ACHIEVED (DEADLINE)

USE ADDITIONAL FORMS AS NEEDED

MPI GOAL PLANNING INSERT, PART 2

INSTRUCTIONS: List the goal numbers from Part 1 and check the current status of each goal. Give evidence for your assessment, including results to date. Use additional forms to set new and/or revised goals.

COMPLETE ALL SECTIONS

Period Ending

GOAL REVIEW

GOAL NUMBER	ACCOMPLISHED	NOT ACCOMPLISHED	PARTIALLY ACCOMPLISHED	UNDETERMINED	EVIDENCE (Results to date)

		Sales Representative	January
No.	Goal Setting	How Measured	When Achieved
1.	Achieve annual sales of $550,000.	Actual orders	March 31 - 25% June 30 - 25% Sept. 30 - 20% Dec. 31 - 30%
2.	Increase distribution of "Big D" deodorant by 50% in *Super Mart, Drug City* and *Stop & Shop*.	Shipments to the stores	Dec. 31
3.	Complete weekly call reports and monthly sales analyses.	The quality of the submitted reports	The Monday following the end of each week and month
4.	Improve relationships with the *Drug City* chain buyers.	Feedback from the customer and site visits	March

Goal Setting

REVIEWING GOALS

Part 2 of the *Goal Planning Insert* can be used to review goals at any time during the year. With clearly defined and frequently reviewed goals, the formal PRD interview becomes an inventory process. The question is, were the goals:

Accomplished?—the project is over, the deadline met, the task completed.

Partially accomplished?—e.g., on sales target for the first two quarters with the annual quota yet to be reached.

Not accomplished?—e.g., relationships with other departments have stayed the same or worsened.

Undetermined?—not enough data, the goal was not stated clearly, or it relates to a fourth quarter activity.

Give evidence to support each judgment.

Though planning for improvement is discussed in detail in Chapter 12, guidelines for reviewing goals are appropriate at this point.

1. Ask each employee for a self-assessment—it's important to obtain the employee's input before offering yours.
2. Reinforce on-target goals—recognize all goals accomplished by the employee and show approval and satisfaction.
3. Identify goals not accomplished—some of these may have been identified by the subordinate. In any case, recount a lack of accomplishment; corroborate your conclusions with facts and figures.
4. Discuss reasons for non-accomplishment—again, ask the employee first.
5. Agree on remedial steps—ask the employee to suggest how to get back on target. Add previously considered solutions. Together, agree on the next steps.
6. Translate the steps into new or revised goals—these should be written out, as were the original goals, with measurement defined and deadlines established.
7. Set a date for the next review. As in goal setting, it's important to express confidence in and support of the employee. To insure that you stay on track, set a mini-review within the next sixty days to monitor progress toward the new goals.

View goals with an *opportunity-oriented attitude*. During the year, conditions emerge that alter priorities (the weight given to each goal), change existing goals and introduce new ones. Use these occurrences to assess the situation and revise expectations.

The "Goal Review" side of the *Goal Planning Insert* highlights an employee's performance. Entries should be brief. For example:

— Sales Representative	Territory covered at 105 percent of budget. (Accomplished)
— District Sales Manager	Filled empty territory in three months and trained a new rep. to be productive. (Partially accomplished)
— Product Manager	Developed a new advertising program that received a Burke of 44. (Accomplished)

— Plant Accountant	In the first six months, did not complete four financial statements on time. Did not analyze, footnote or explain variances. (Not accomplished)
— Shift Supervisor	Scrappage was increased by 8 percent. (Not accomplished)
— Warehouse General Foreman	Storage capacity was increased by implementing "double deep" racking. (Accomplished)

One drawback of writing in detail about job responsibilities and goals is that they appear cumbersome and overwhelming. On the contrary, I believe that these preparatory steps (defining responsibilities and setting goals) make assessments easier and more objective, and they prevent later misunderstandings and disagreements. Until you can describe a job clearly and precisely, you cannot rate the person performing that job.

APPLICATION AND REVIEW

1. Identify five sources of help in defining the job.

    (a)

    (b)

    (c)

    (d)

    (e)

2. Place the following goals in the matrix below:
    a. Achieve 47 percent of market share.
    b. Insure that all safety procedures are followed during satellite launches.
    c. Remain calm when dealing with union representatives over a potential grievance.
    d. Type six letters per day.
    e. Resolve problems created by changing production schedules.
    f. Keep a neat work area when waiting on customers.

GOALS	METHODS	RESULTS
Simple		
Complex		
Crisis		

3. If you *haven't* set goals before, try doing it for one of your employees. If you *have* written goals, rate them against the six criteria, which are:

    (a)

    (b)

    (c)

    (d)

    (e)

    (f)

4. Briefly list the eight guidelines for *setting* goals.

   (a)

   (b)

   (c)

   (d)

   (e)

   (f)

   (g)

   (h)

5. Briefly list the seven guidelines for *reviewing* goals.

   (a)

   (b)

   (c)

   (d)

   (e)

   (f)

   (g)

SUGGESTED RESPONSES

1. Job descriptions, other managers, your superior, your current subordinates, and past outstanding performances in the job.

2.

	Method	Result
Simple	F	D
Complex	B	A
Crisis	C	E

3. Clarity, realism, consistency, control, challenge, and efficacy.

4. (a) Employee submits goals.
    (b) Formulate goals.
    (c) Communicate goals.
    (d) Modify and agree.
    (e) Discuss action and commitment.
    (f) Establish measures and deadlines.
    (g) Employee summarizes.
    (h) Express confidence and set review date.

5. (a) Employee assesses self.
    (b) Reinforce on-target goals.
    (c) Identify goals not accomplished.
    (d) Discuss reason for non-accomplishment.
    (e) Agree on remedial steps.
    (f) Set new goals.
    (g) Set next review.

CHAPTER 6

DOCUMENTATION

"Why didn't you review this with me in June instead of December 31. I can't change things now."

"Where does it say that? Show me in writing."

As well as acting as a reporter of job behavior, the manager has to be a *recorder*. This implies paperwork (and considerable lamentation). None of us wants more log work, but we need systematic records and accuracy. If that requires additional paper, so be it.

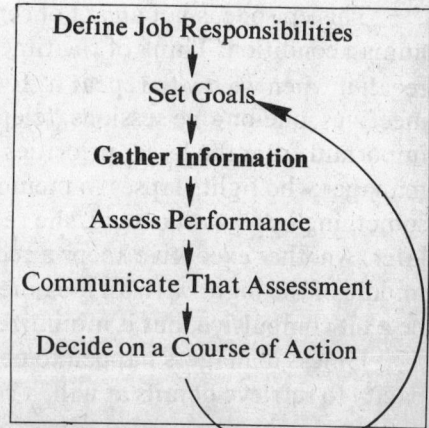

Define Job Responsibilities

↓

Set Goals

↓

Gather Information

↓

Assess Performance

↓

Communicate That Assessment

↓

Decide on a Course of Action

RATIONALE FOR DOCUMENTATION

Three reasons for documenting an employee's performance are:
Poor Memory. We are known to have notoriously bad memories. Consider this testimony of a typical manager:

> Last fall driving to the office, a solution to a problem I had been working
> on flashed clearly in mind. Five minutes later in my office, I sat down to
> write out the solution. Just then the telephone rang, triggering a series of
> events that occupied my time until 8:00 pm. I proceeded to course my way
> through the day, using a *zigzag method of management.* Driving to work
> the next morning at about the same spot, I remembered the idea—that is, I
> remembered I had had an idea, but I could not reconstruct it. I tried recall-
> ing it by association. When I got to the office I attempted to diagram it,
> but, in the end, it was lost.

This episode is not an act of senility, but, rather, is representative of the
human condition. Think of the times we hear a good story, but are unable to
recall it when we try to repeat it. Every hour we are besieged by stimuli —
meetings, one-on-one sessions, telephone calls, memos, mail. Sorting out the
important from the lesser priorities becomes a complex cerebral task. I know a
manager who fights lapses in memory with a small pocket recorder. When
something important occurs, she records it immediately, then transcribes it
later. Another executive keeps a recorder at bedside; when he awakens in the
middle of the night with an idea, he records it and goes back to sleep. This may
be a bit compulsive, but it minimizes the frustration of forgetfulness.

Unless managers happen to possess that rare gift of great writers, the capacity to retrieve details at will, a running account of the production of employees should be recorded. Research suggests that familiar surroundings help
one recall events that occurred there. If a manager has jotted brief notes and
wants to recall more, walking around the work area can jar memories and help
him or her retrieve the particulars of an employee's performance.

Professional Management. Becoming more systematic in supervising
people is just plain sound management. Intuition has a definite function in decision-making, but intuitive solutions do not emanate from a vacuum. Intuition is frequently derived from a mass of previously ingested information.
Recording that data minimizes the mystery of decisions, because printed history can be studied and learned from.

In Chapter 3, I introduced two concepts:

- The appraisal continuum—thinking about performance in 12-month
  blocks, rather than discrete events or snapshots.
- Managing on the run—collecting and assessing information, giving
  positive and negative feedback, and suggesting new courses of action
  periodically, as an employee's performance (or lack thereof) dictates.

A performance *mural* is drawn over time, presenting a series of interlocking

ZIG-ZAG MANAGEMENT

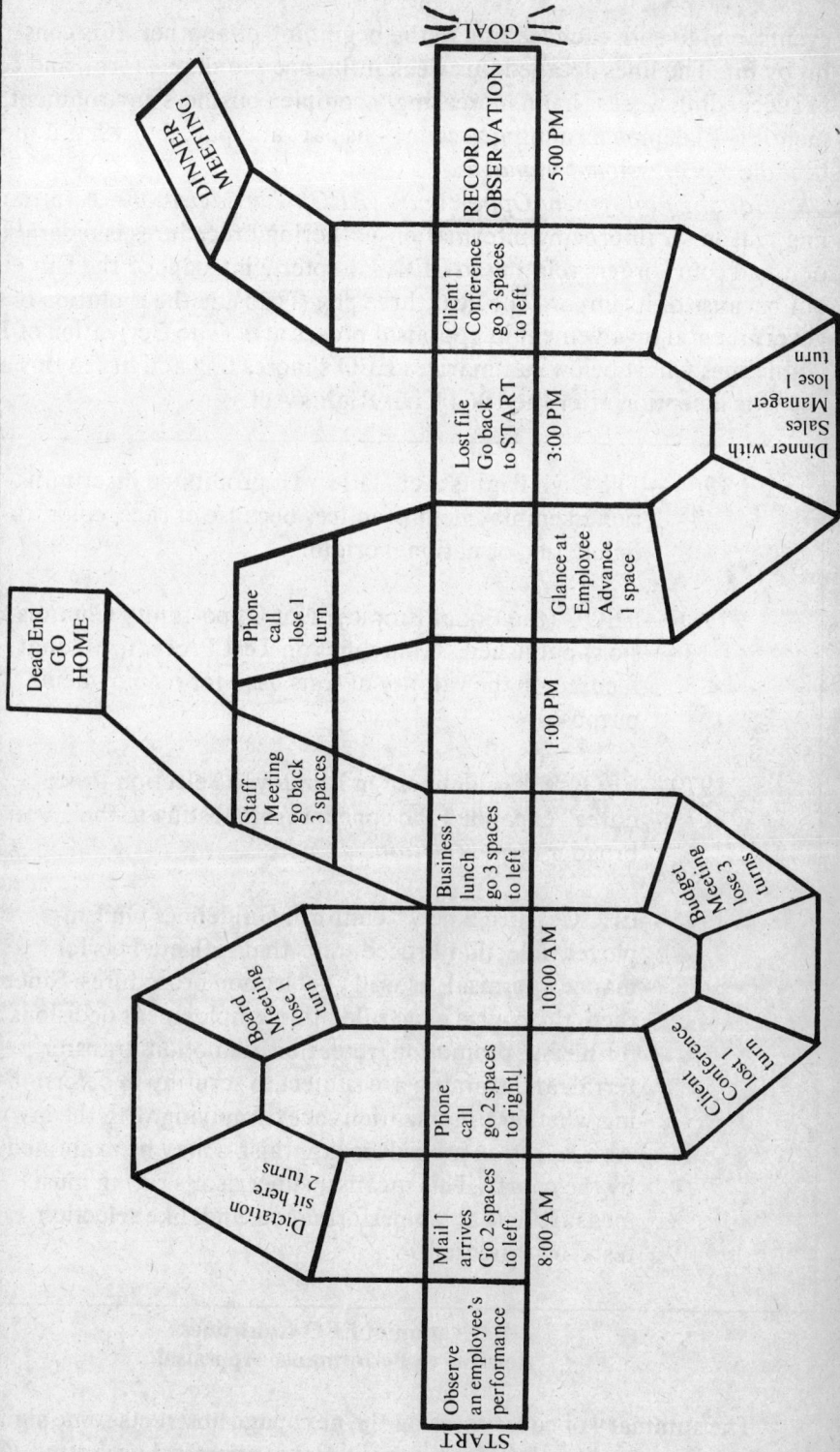

START

Observe an employee's performance

8:00 AM

Mail — Go 2 spaces to left

Dictation sit here 2 turns

Phone call go 2 spaces to right

Board Meeting lose 1 turn

10:00 AM

Client Conference lost 1 turn

Budget Meeting lose 3 turns

Business — lunch go 3 spaces to left

Staff Meeting go back 3 spaces

Dead End GO HOME

Phone call lose 1 turn

1:00 PM

Glance at Employee Advance 1 space

Lost file Go back to START

3:00 PM

Dinner with Sales Manager lose 1 turn

Client — Conference go 3 spaces to left

DINNER MEETING

RECORD OBSERVATION

5:00 PM

GOAL

events, end to end, each leading to the beginning of another. It is constructed bit by bit. The lines detailed this week influence the shape, form, and contours of succeeding weeks. In an increasingly complex business environment, documenting—keeping a running account—is part and parcel of what it means to become a *professional manager*.

Equal Employment Opportunity (EEO) Considerations. A third compelling reason for improving information-gathering procedures is federal legislation and court orders relating to EEO. Chapter 2 introduced the EEO issue, but because of its import, the next three pages capsule the evolution of governmental involvement in appraisal procedures. The Derivation of EEO Guidelines Chart below summarizes EEO's increasing activity in this area since its inception after the 1964 Civil Rights Act.

1964—The Civil Rights Act, Title VII, prohibited discrimination in employment practices because of race, color, religion, sex, or national origin.

1966—EEOC (the Equal Employment Opportunity Commission) published "Guidelines on Test Procedures" that focused on the validity of tests used for employment purposes.

1970—EEOC's "Guidelines On Employee Selection Procedures" expanded the concept from testing to the broader term *selection*.

1978—EEOC issued a new "Uniform Guidelines On Employee Selection Procedures" that reflected performance appraisal, as well as selection procedures. Since then, the courts have ruled that employment decisions for hiring, promotion, retention, demotion, transfer, referral, and training are subject to scrutiny in determining whether organizations are complying with the law. As a *selection* procedure, appraisals may be examined by the courts. This means a supervisor's rating must measure actual job performance, and, like selection tests, be validated.

**Derivation of EEO Guidelines
Relating to Performance Appraisal**

The summary of court cases on the next page abstracts some significant legal rulings that directly affect organizational appraisal programs. (See also

Lubben, Thompson, and Klasson's "Performance Appraisal: The Legal Implications of Title VII" in *Personnel*, May-June 1980.)

- *Griggs v. Duke Power* (1971)—Among other things, the court ruled that the validity of the use of intelligence tests and high school diplomas as requirements for a job could not be proven. And, since they excluded blacks, they were discriminatory.

- *Rowe v. General Motors Corporation* (1972)—The court ruled that the GMC promotion/transfer system was in violation of Title VII, because it was primarily based on supervisor recommendations, which were found to be subjective. Also, supervisors received no written instruction on the qualifications necessary for promotion.

- *United States v. N. L. Industries* (1973)—The company was charged with discrimination because it permitted supervisors to choose from a list of persons eligible for promotion, without the use of a standard. Ratings were applied differently for black than for white employees. The court ordered the company to design an efficiency-rating system to eliminate the discriminatory effects.

- *Brito v. Zia Company* (1973)—Brito maintained that a disproportionate number of Hispanic employees were laid off based on low performance appraisal scores. The court ruled that Zia did not validate its performance evaluation instrument—there were no identifiable criteria based on quality or quantity of work. It is a landmark case because the court decided that a performance appraisal is a test, and, as such, must be validated.

- *Baxter v. Savannah Refining Corporation* (1974)—In a situation similar to the GMC case, the court ordered the company to provide supervisors with written instructions specifying the criteria necessary for promotion.

- *Wade v. Mississippi Cooperative Extension Service* (1974)—The court held that the Extension Service had the burden of demonstrating that an evaluation instrument used to appraise the performance of county professional workers was job related and served legitimate employment needs. Wade maintained that it discriminated against black employees; the court stated that this claim must be negated "by clear and convincing evidence." One key criterion used for determining promotion was an "objective appraisal of job performance." Finding against the Extension Service, the court concluded that this "objective" appraisal evaluated such general characteristics as leadership, attitude, appearance, personal conduct, outlook on life, ethical habits, resourcefulness, capacity for growth, mental alertness, and loyalty which are susceptible to partiality and the whim or fancy of the evaluator.

- *Albermarle v. Moody* (1975)—As mentioned in Chapter 2, the court judged that appraisal ratings represent subjective human judgments and are discriminatory if: based on ill-defined criteria, affected by sexual or racial bias, not standardized, not based on a careful job analysis, or if not validated.

- *Rogers v. International Paper Company* (1976)—The first recognition that a performance appraisal cannot be totally objective. The court indicated that subjective criteria are not unlawful per se, unless they represent the major criteria used for rating an employee.

Summary of Court Cases

The number of recent court cases provides ample evidence that appraisals are receiving more and more EEO scrutiny. This "public attention" demands that managers:

(a) Write explicit job descriptions
(b) Define measurable standards
(c) Collect and record representative performance data
(d) Match the performance to the *job* standards
(e) Give employees frequent feedback on their performance

Should an employee file a complaint, the organization is presumed guilty (prima facie case) until it demonstrates that its appraisal system is directly related to job performance (test of validity).

Therefore, EEO, a natural forgetfulness, and good management techniques necessitate that managers *document* the progress of employees.

1. Pick a job position that you are responsible for supervising:
2. List the criteria for judging the person in this position (may be the same as your list in Chapter 1). If these are not pre-set on your appraisal form, write your own.

3. For each of the preceding criteria, determine the answers to the following questions:
    (a) Is the criterion based on a job analysis?
    (b) Do your colleagues and superiors agree that the criterion is essential to the job?
    (c) Can you demonstrate from past and current experience that failure to meet this criterion adversely affects job performance?
4. What are the sources of information on which you base your performance appraisals?

SAMPLING

Sampling is a way of life. We sample everything from soup to public opinion. On November 4, 1980, residents of California knew Ronald Reagan had been elected President, even before their voting booths had closed. Why? Because TV pollsters had carefully hand selected a small number of voters (mostly east of the Mississippi), representative of the socio-economic-political levels of the total voter population, recorded their votes, and projected the results, taking advantage of the three-hour East-West time difference. Sampling allows us to take one swallow of wine, and, with confidence, predict what the rest of the bottle is like.

A sample, then, is a smaller replica of the whole. A product manager determines the acceptability of a new product by the reactions of a random (unbiased) sampling of consumers. The probability that the manager will be right depends on how adequate and how representative the sample tested actually is. Not all populations of people, things or behaviors are as easily sampled as blood and wine. For instance, take job performance. Gathering information about an employee's actions poses a variety of problems:

— The manager can't observe the individual in all job situations.
— Behaviors (good vs. bad) may not have an equal chance of being observed (see Notions 6, 15, and 16 in Chapter 1).
— Observer error can result in certain data being selected to the exclusion of other information, e.g., an abrasive manner sometimes erases the success of several projects.
— A busy manager may see an employee very little.
— The manager can misinterpret the behavior sample.

Example Behavior:	An employee sitting with his feet on the desk.
Interpretation:	He's loafing.
Actual:	The subordinate is thinking through ways to reduce late shipments to customers.

Example Behavior:	An employee is always first to work and last to leave.
Interpretation:	A hard worker, "a good company man."
Actual:	The employee accomplishes very little, but "keeps his nose clean."

Managers can enhance the reliability of appraisals by increasing their observations and seeking multiple sources of data. More specifically, the manager can:

- *Select a purposive sample*—that is, select aspects of the job that are typical, e.g., technical *and* interpersonal, routine *and* complex.
- *Time sample*—schedule observations (directly or indirectly collected data), to cover a variety of job situations—i.e., low/high pressure, morning/afternoon, beginning/end of the quarter.
- *Personally observe the work of an employee*—e.g., traveling with a sales representative. Direct observation can be impressive, but not without limitation. For one, employees may perform differently under

observation than when they are alone. Reps. out to impress the boss can easily set up appointments with clients who will make them look good. Or, some employees "clutch" and do not perform well when the boss is looking over their shoulders. A second limitation is time—the time it takes to observe behavior directly. In many situations, regular "site visits" may be impractical.

- *Work with the employee*—on a project or problem as a co-worker. This gives the manager an opportunity to rub elbows with the subordinate, to be an interested participant rather than just a dispassionate observer.

- *Collect recurrent data on goal attainment*—If clear outcomes have been established, managers can determine whether goals are achieved without observing actual performance: e.g., sales figures, reports, absenteeism or scrappage rates. To repeat: management by results is desirable, but not all jobs lend themselves to quantifiable outcomes. In such cases, procedures and approach must be observed.

- *Keep periodic notations on discussions with the employee*—based on weekly conversations with the employee or on activity in staff meetings.

- *Keep anecdotal records*—One form is the critical incident technique, consisting of descriptions of behavior in specific job situations that clearly document successes and failures when they occur: e.g., a supervisor motivates a malingering employee to perform extra tasks, or a sales rep. fails to respond to a customer's request to remove damaged goods.

Anecdotes are an outstanding way to record examples of performance, but they take time to write and are hard to quantify and rate. Actually, the writing can be simplified. A Critical Incident Card is a running log on 3x5 cards carried in a pocket or purse. When an episode occurs, the manager records it in a few words, along with the date and the job responsibility/goal/task to which it relates. The performance is rated and the employee is given immediate feedback. The entire process should take no longer than a few minutes *(managing on the run, again!)*.

Job Responsibility	Date	Episode	Goal	Rating	Feedback Given
Major Projects:					
Day-to-Day Activities:					

Critical Incident Card

Another example is the Cumulative Anecdotal Record. Incidents are put in columns according to their success or failure. Note that the performances need not be observed directly. Some will, but many will show up in analyses or be reported by others. Over a three- to six-month period, these incidents are deposited into a memory bank to be drawn on during the formal appraisal.

Employee's Name *F. McCumkaill*   Position *Supervisor*

1981 Date	Unsatisfactory Incidents	Satisfactory Incidents	Date
10/26	Refused to try a new procedure	Helped Charlie with his overtime problem	9/15
11/18	Late to work	Met MPI production schedule despite equipment problems	10/1
		Trained new employee in safety regulations	12/3

Cumulative Anecdotal Record

- Collect the reactions of others—colleagues, superiors, the employee's peers, personnel from other departments, customers. Their views can be acquired informally by listening to the way an employee's peers relate to him/her, and by reading between the lines; or, more formally, by systematically surveying the judgments of customers or other personnel close to the employee.

These eight techniques can increase the reliability of performance information by helping managers become more systematic as data gatherers, by increasing the quantity and quality of information, and by extending the sources of that information.

Are the behaviors that form the basis of your assessment a representative sample of the employee's work?

Representative means:

a) They are *relevant* to the job being performed (rather than personal).

b) They *encompass* job behavior throughout the rating period.

c) Their *weight* corresponds to the importance assigned to each job responsibility and goal.

d) They *adequately* illustrate quality as well as quantity of work.

PARSIMONY

Gathering information about an employee's performance requires thought and pre-design, but documentation need not overwhelm managers if they follow the principle of PARSIMONY. *Multum in parvo,* or much in little, means drawing a picture with a few words. Even checklists need instances of performance to help explain and expand them. Consider the following suggestions:

- **Write Specifically.** Avoid generalities like "he's lazy" or "she's got no motivation" or "she's doing a fine job." Specify the derivation for these conclusions. *Why* lazy? *Why* unmotivated? *Why* a fine job? What's the evidence?
- **Show, Rather than Tell.** In place of writing "MacCumhaill gets along well with workers," relate a model incident: e.g., the shop steward spontaneously exclaiming, "MacCumhaill is one of your top supervisors. It's a pleasure to work with him."

- **Use Pithy Phrases.** Instead of long *crocodilean* sentences like "He/she frequently approaches a project with little preparation and prior thinking about a strategic plan of action," try "her projects hunger for planning" or "scrimpy project planning."
- **Use Adjectives and Adverbs Sparingly.** "He did a beautiful job" and "she is very good" are not useful because they contain unclear value statements. The word *good* might mean "super," but with a different inflexion means "OK, barely acceptable." Because of their ambiguity, evaluative adjectives and adverbs may describe any level of achievement from *average* to *outstanding*. Better to directly relate the particulars of success or failure, and let the rating indicate whether the incident constituted positive, comparative, or superlative performance.
- **Balance Positives with Negatives.** The tendency is to detail negatives over positives, blowing them out of proportion. They then occupy more space in the records, thus assuming greater importance. The *Cumulative Anecdotal Record* on page 95 indicates one way to ensure that successes and failures are recorded and kept in perspective. Another way to achieve balance is to compliment employees daily on tasks performed well. This recognition reinforces desired behavior and increases the probability that it will be repeated. It also lays a solid base for discussing and dealing with substandard performance.

Below, some general statements are translated into specifics. Complete the list by writing in your own examples.

General	Specific
— She did a nice job	— Sold new promotion to *Big-Y Drugs*.
— He's a hard worker	— Worked nights and weekends to complete the analysis of the new compensation program.
— He motivates his people	— Assigned added work to a trouble-maker and he willingly completed it.
— He has a bad attitude	—
— She plans ahead	—
— He's an enthusiastic employee	—
— She gets along well with others	—
— He procrastinates	—

Ideas on Documenting Performance

— Complete a precise, written job analysis.
— Weigh job responsibilities and goals according to impor-
  tance.
— Provide timely feedback immediately following the
  performance.
— Record incidents of and communiqués about
  performance.
— Keep a *running* record.
— Note specific examples of performance.
— Be parsimonious in writing.
— Record job-related data.
— Interact frequently with those whom you assess.
— Insure that the files adequately portray effective and inef-
  fective performance, the employee's strengths as well as
  weaknesses.
— Represent the employee's total performance—all respon-
  sibilities and goals over the entire rating period.
— Seek other people's assessment of the employee.
— Standardize data-gathering procedures.
— Seek training to upgrade skills in conducting appraisals.

I am not talking about documentation to protect oneself (though it may indeed do that), but rather documenting in the Latin sense—*docere* meaning *to teach*.
of, but it is not now and never has been a consistently effective way to get the job done. Managers must systematically track and record work progress:

— Defensively, to satisfy a minimum EEO requirement that levels of
  performance be documented in the employee's file
      and
— Offensively, to provide a job history for analysis and future decision
  making.

A brief, but representative, written record charts:

— What's happening on the job.
— Where the employee stands.
— What recognition should be given.
— What changes need to be made.
— What steps are necessary to improve performance.

APPLICATION AND REVIEW

1. Three reasons for upgrading performance records are:

    (a)

    (b)

    (c)

2. List at least five sources of information on the performance of employees:

    (a)

    (b)

    (c)

    (d)

    (e)

3. Four criteria for judging the fairness of your sample of job performances are:

    (a)

    (b)

    (c)

    (d)

4. *Parsimony* refers to:

5. In addition to collecting and recording, *documentation* also implies:

6. From your experience and the discussion in this chapter, jot down three ways you can improve the data upon which you base your appraisals:

    (a)

    (b)

    (c)

SUGGESTED RESPONSES

1. Good management practice, EEO, and as compensation for memory lapses.
2. Direct observation, data on results, communication with the employee, working side by side with the employee, reactions of others.
3. (a) Is it relevant to the job?
   (b) Does it encompass the total rating period?
   (c) Is it weighted according to job responsibilities and goals?
   (d) Does it adequately illustrate the quality and quantity of work?
4. Being stingy with words, compressing them to conserve recording time and to chronicle a graphic account of performance.
5. Teaching.
6. Answers will vary.

CHAPTER 7

RATING THE PERFORMANCE

"I disagree with your assessment."
"I don't care what you say. *Competent* is average. I'm not an average person."
"Why wasn't that project *outstanding* instead of *satisfactory*?"
"Can you tell me the difference between *Achieves* and *Excels*, specifically in terms of job performance?"
"Interpersonal relations is not a measurable quantity."

All of the above quotations aim at *ratings*, not *assessment*, which is the fourth phase of PRD. Since, in the field, the two are frequently used synonymously, and since most appraisal systems require ratings, I have chosen to entitle this chapter "*Rating* the Performance." The following topics are covered in order:

(a) The relationship between PRD, assessment and ratings
(b) The persistence of ratings
(c) The complexities in rating performance
(d) Some suggested procedures

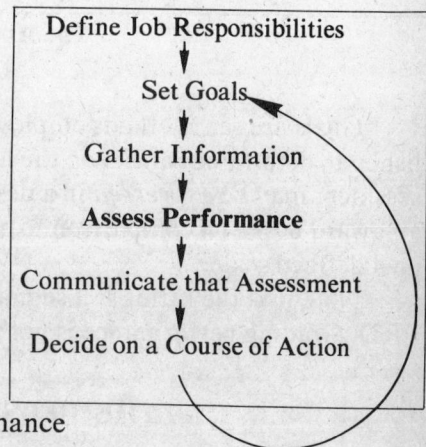

Define Job Responsibilities
↓
Set Goals
↓
Gather Information
↓
Assess Performance
↓
Communicate that Assessment
↓
Decide on a Course of Action

RELATIONSHIP BETWEEN PRD, ASSESSMENT, AND RATINGS

In previous chapters, *Performance Review and Development* (PRD) has been defined as a total system for determining if a job is being performed well, and, in cases when it is not, for taking corrective steps. PRD *is* performance appraisal.

Assessment represents but one of six PRD elements. Using information from Chapter 3, assessment is illustrated by the pyramid on the next page.

Methods   Measurement

(a)   Job   (b)

Results

Goals

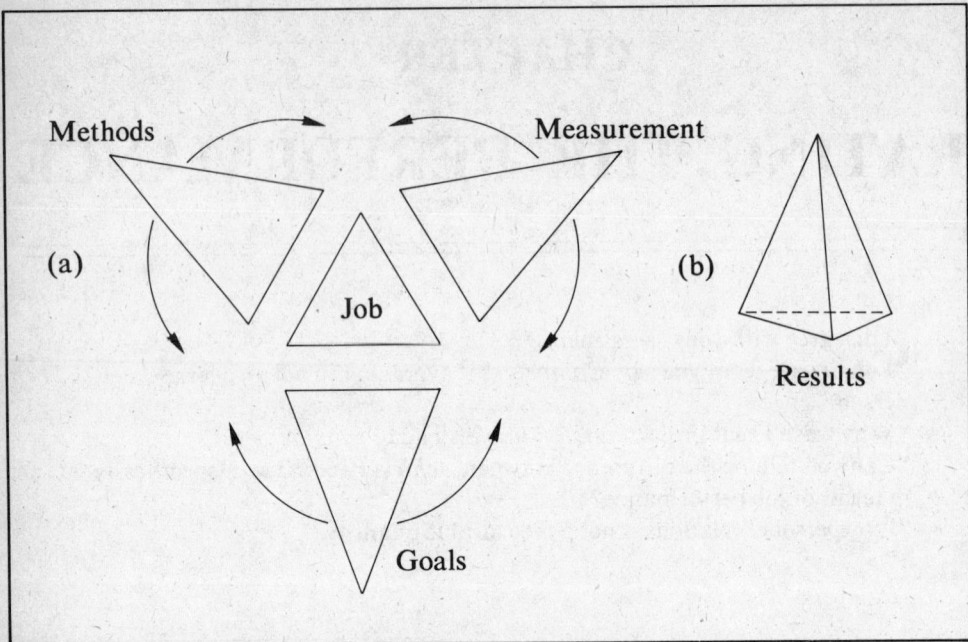

The Assessment Pyramid

Goals are set, methods employed, and a means of measurement is established to determine *results* on the level of success in a particular job. This assessment may be *expressed* in a descriptive statement, a face-to-face dialogue, an award based on comparison to others in the same position, and/or a *rating* on a defined scale.

Note that the rating is a segment of assessment that is a subdivision of PRD. Grading performance is not mandatory. It just is.

THE PERSISTENCE OF RATINGS

Why do we rate the performance of employees? First we are conditioned to grades by our educational system. Advancing from one school level to another requires a minimum grade average. Similarly, employees expect and even demand to be rated. Second, salary administration is so designed that ratings are necessary to place employees at different points on the salary scale. Third, ratings are used to compare personnel for promotion purposes. Finally, in some cases, ratings persist just because it's always been done that way.

Psychologically, ratings tend to work against employee development (see Notion 1 in Chapter 1). Grades encourage employees to do only those things that visibly contribute to high marks, some of which may work against a quality job. Students learn to memorize useless information for a test, then forget it the next day. Employees do the same: they "*psych out*" the bosses and act to impress them. However, improved performance may depend more on analysis and action than on pleasing employers. The two objectives, development and satisfying the manager, sometimes conflict. For instance, an employee may not venture new ideas for fear of displeasing the boss.

PRD primarily aims at the productivity issue, and, as such, doesn't require a scaled rating. But the realities of the business world dictate grades. Since ratings persist, what are some different approaches? An example of diversity in grading occurred when I was a student at Stanford University. One quarter I was enrolled in four courses, and each had its own marking system:

Psychology—a 1-3 scale, with 3 the top grade, but none of the numbers defined.

Sociology—a 125 point scale with no indication of what 100 meant (or 85 or 50 for that matter).

Statistics—100 points based on ten problems, each worth 10 points. If a student computed the wrong answer (outcome) but showed a logical step-by-step thought process (methodology), the professor would mark the problem 10-minus. Theoretically, the student could turn in 10 wrong answers, yet score 100 (with ten minuses). Effort and understanding obviously counted along with the end product.

Independent research—three grades: unsatisfactory, satisfactory, superior.

Organizations, like universities, exhibit a variety of sometimes ill-defined rating systems. Assigning work, gathering information, and describing performance are difficult enough tasks. Even more complex is categorizing that performance along a continuum from bad to good.

Examples of a 2-point (goals achieved/ not achieved), 5-point, and 15-point scale, plus an open-ended "zero scale" essay format were shown in Chapter 4 (Figures 10-13). Additional ones are pictured on succeeding pages. (For a detailed discussion of rating systems, see The Conference Board's *Appraising Managerial Performance. Current Practices and Future Directions,* 1977.)

The next page illustrates three *graphic* scales — a 4-point, 10-point, and 200-point scale.

1. Relationship with Subordinates

1 2	3 4	5 6	7 8	9 10
Does not get along. Ignores concerns of employees.	Sometimes overlooks need for co-operation. Area for improvement.	Satisfactory relationships. Usually co-operative.	Superior in cooperation. Accepted by others. Few disputes.	Exceptional relationships Well liked.

Performance Ratings	Final Rating
2.0 Outstanding	D = 170+
1.5 Excels	E = 130-170
1.0 Achieves	A = 90-130
0.5 Needs Improvement	NI = 50-90
0.0 Unsatisfactory	U = 50−

Job Responsibilities	(1) Weight (Total=100)	(2) Performance Rating	Total (1)x(2)
1.			
2.			
3.			
4.			
		Total Points	
		Final Rating	

Performance Objectives	4 Exceeds OBJ	3 Achieves OBJ	2 Falls Short in some OBJ	1 Unsatis-factory
1. Operates within affirmative action plans.				
2. Achieves safety standards				
3. Meets deadlines				

Three Rating Scales

As discussed in Chapter 1, a behavior scale lists a set of behaviors developed out of an analysis of jobs in the organization. The manager gauges the behavior that most represents the employee's execution. Two examples follow—one, a 6-point behaviorally anchored rating scale (BARS), and the other, a *most-least* forced-choice comparison of sets of behavior.

Superior Performance	6-	Knows the strengths and weaknesses of all subordinates and assists and supports them in improving their performance. Demonstrates unique, on-the-job training techniques.
Excellent Performance	5-	Meets with subordinates at least 4 times a year to assess progress toward goals. Knows where they are at all times.
Above Average Performance	4-	In emergencies, works overtime with subordinates to help them solve problems.
Average Performance	3-	Completes annual appraisal; subordinates perform acceptably but show no appreciable improvement.
Below Average Performance	2-	Seldom recognizes subordinates' accomplishments. Gives negative feedback under pressure, but does not follow through.
Unacceptable Performance	1-	Always critical of subordinates; does nothing to help them improve.

Behavioral Rating Scale

Indicate which of the following statements is most like and least like the employee by checking (✔) the appropriate column.

Most   *Least*

( )   ( )   Gets along well with colleagues.

( )   ( )   Fails to prepare for presentations.

( )   ( )   Considers the ideas of others.

( )   ( )   Does not get flustered under deadline pressures.

( )   ( )   Gives credit to others when they perform well.

Forced Choice Comparison

Two rank order approaches are shown here. The first is simply a list of names of employees performing similar tasks. The manager compares their overall performance by ranking them from first to last. The second illustrates a paired comparison system called the Objective Judgment Quotient (OJQ), developed by Wyvern Research Associates, Sausalito, California. In OJQ several managers rate employees against each other on each of several predetermined criteria. A computer printout provides profiles with ranks and scores on each criterion, the standing of an individual within the group, and a consensus evaluation.

Employee to be Ranked	Rank Order
J. Conners	1 Highest performer:
R. Woods	2 Next Highest:
C. Mapleton	3 Next Highest:

First Rank Order Approach

Check one of the boxes for each pairing of the following people:

SELLING SKILLS

	Much Better	Somewhat Better	About Equal	Somewhat Better	Much Better	
J. Conners	[ ]	[ ]	[ ]	[ ]	[ ]	R. Woods
C. Mapleton	[ ]	[ ]	[ ]	[ ]	[ ]	J. Conners
R. Woods	[ ]	[ ]	[ ]	[ ]	[ ]	C. Mapleton

PRODUCT KNOWLEDGE

J. Conners	[ ]	[ ]	[ ]	[ ]	[ ]	R. Woods
C. Mapleton	[ ]	[ ]	[ ]	[ ]	[ ]	J. Conners
R. Woods	[ ]	[ ]	[ ]	[ ]	[ ]	C. Mapleton

Second Rank Order Approaches

Compare the rating system in your organization to the examples. Which comes closest to yours? Take a recent appraisal of a subordinate, and, on your criteria, rate that employee using one of the scales presented here. Compare the results with your original rating.

COMPLEXITIES IN RATING PERFORMANCE

The variety of instruments suggests the search for more objective measurement. The PRD form (Chapter 4) has three ratings: outstanding, competent, and marginal. Most managers can identify their outstanding and less-than-satisfactory performers. Employees in-between are performing competently, some to a greater degree than others, but finely-tuned discriminations may be indefensible and unreliable. For some of the scales on the previous pages, try to distinguish between a level 4 performance and a 5, 6 or 7. If you saw a 3 performer and a 4 performer working side by side, how would you tell the difference?

To test the charge that you cannot distinguish between ratings such as *excels* and *achieves,* try this experiment with your current rating scale:

- Eliminate the high (e.g., outstanding) and low (e.g., marginal) ratings.
- List the remaining grades in the left hand column below.
- Opposite each rating, note the job behaviors that clearly describe the rating.

Rating	Description of Job Performance
(1)	
(2)	
(3)	
(4)	

Ask one or more of your colleagues to do the same, and compare the results. I doubt that you will agree on what distinguishes performance for each level. The same descriptions for one grade show up for another.

On the opposite page is a humorous but vivid attempt to differentiate between ratings on five criteria.

Does this mean no rating scale should have more than three intervals? Of course not. Larger scales can show the subtlety and strength of a rater's attitude. And frequently, a rating tells more about the rater than the ratee. In assessment, there is a general or "*G-factor*" at work—that is, the items on a scale are probably not as powerful as the preset attitudes and biases of the rater. For instance, managers put "halos" on their favorite subordinates or "dunce caps" on trouble-makers, and evaluate employees within those expectations. (See examples on page 110) This distortion of reality can have harmful effects on the good worker as well as the poor one if the manager is unaware that it exists. The G-factor can result in:

- An unfair rating
- Subsequent subpar performance
- Deterioration of boss-subordinate relations

Rating scales and their use in assessment present some complex issues for serious thought. If managers cannot designate discrete sets of job behaviors for each rating, they should question the reliability of the ratings. They are questionable as a general management practice, questionable in their fairness to employees, and questionable by EEO standards.

BEHAVIOR DEFINITIONS FOR A 5-POINT PERFORMANCE RATING SCALE

PERFORMANCE TASK	5. OUTSTANDING	4. EXCELLENT	3. COMPETENT	2. MARGINAL	1. DISPOSABLE
Overcomes Obstacles to Achieving Goals	Leaps tall buildings in a single bound	Must take running start to leap tall buildings	Can leap over short buildings only	Crashes into buildings when attempting to leap over them	Cannot recognize buildings at all
Meets Deadlines	Faster than a speeding bullet	As fast as a speeding bullet	Not quite as fast as a speeding bullet	Would you believe a slow bullet	Wounds self with bullet when attempting to shoot
Leads by Example	Stronger than a locomotive	Stronger than a bull elephant	Stronger than a bull	Shoots the bull	Smells like a bull
Handles Pressure Situations	Walks on water consistently	Walks on water in emergencies	Washes with water	Drinks water	Passes water in a crises
Practices 2-way Communication	Communicates with God	Communicates with the angels	Talks to self	Argues with self	Loses arguments with self

(Source Unknown)

Research has demonstrated one's perceptions are influenced by expectations or mental set. In one study, teachers were deliberately misinformed about the abilities of their pupils. In each of the school's 18 classrooms, an average of 20 percent of the children, randomly selected, were reported to the teacher as showing, as a result of an IQ test, "unusual" potential for intellectual gains. Eight months later, these "unusual" children showed significantly greater gains in IQ than the remaining pupils in the class. One implication of this study: if a teacher thought a pupil was intelligent, he or she behaved in such a way that the pupil became or appeared intelligent.

This same kind of research has been conducted in business and industry. Supervisors were told that certain members of a new work team had "great potential" (when in fact their work history was one of malingering). After working together, the supervisors typically rated the "great potential" employees as the best performers.

In another study, managers and workers were given pictures and descriptions of an "ordinary" person. The descriptions were varied in only one item—in half the descriptions the person was described as a *manager of a small plant;* in the other half, as *secretary-treasurer of his union.* The rest of the descriptions were identical. Managers and hourly workers evaluated the "described man" on 290 personality traits. The result was that managers generally rated the "plant manager" description much higher than the "Union secretary-treasurer" description. Workers rated the "Union secretary-treasurer" much higher than the "plant manager." The general impression of the person was radically different when he was seen as a member of management than when he was seen as a representative of labor.

Examples of the "G-Factor"

What are some other complex issues in rating employees?

- *Task Difficulty*— How are lesser tasks balanced with difficult ones? How does "record-keeping" compare with "managing the territory," or partial success on a complex project vs. total success on a simple assignment?
- *Task Visibility*—Lesser accomplishments may be highly visible, while significant contributions go unnoticed. A fine fielding second baseman may be overshadowed by a mediocre fielding homerun hitter, yet a po-

rous infield loses more games than a homerun can win.

- *Task Predictability*—Achieving 47 percent of market is less certain than maintaining an 8-per-day call average.
- *Task Interdependence*—How do managers rate individuals when their output depends on the performance of other people—another department, staff support, outside suppliers, or other locations?
- *Cause and Effect*—With unpredictable tasks, it's difficult to determine the employee's contribution. If a sales rep makes 120 percent of quota, was it due entirely to his/her efforts? What about windfalls, an economic upturn, or an unusual expansion of customers in the district? Quotas are a function of potentialities as well as realities.
- *Multiple Contributions*—How does the manager rate an individual when more than one person contributes to the end result? (e.g., a sales rep, account manager, and district manager all calling on the same customer.)
- *Availability of Data*—Frequently, more data is available on negative performance than on positive.
- *Uncontrollable Circumstances*—How does the manager rate employees when their performance is affected by circumstances out of their control, e.g., lack of materials or equipment breakdowns. A computer programmer can't debug programs if the machines are constantly out of repair.
- *Unclear Standards*—Rating employees on unclear or nonexisting goals is frequently practiced, but obviously unfair.
- *Inappropriate Standards*—For instance, setting unattainable expectations can justly be called the *blue sky* syndrome.
- *Conflicting Criteria*—A good example is the quality vs. quantity dilemma: "Get it done right and get it done fast!"

PROCEDURES

Short of eliminating rating systems, how does the manager cope with these complex issues? Here are some suggestions for arriving at ratings:

(1) Note your "G-Factor" rating and set it aside. This is your Belly Button Reaction (BBR) to the employee's performance, your assessment before analyzing the data. (See the author's *Managing The Interview,* John Wiley & Sons, 1980, pp. 92–93.)

(2) Together with colleagues, superiors, and subordinates, draw a consensus word description of the key behaviors and accomplishments for each rating (outstanding, competent, marginal, or whatever).

(3) List all accomplishments, and match them up to the agreed-upon goals.

(4) Note gaps in performance, goals not accomplished or only partially fulfilled.

(5) Relate the goal analysis to the proper job responsibility and determine at what level the responsibility was carried out.

(6) Cross check ratings with such performance tasks as knowing the job, managing the job and dealing with people on the job.

(7) Average all ratings, keeping in mind the priorities established when the job responsibilities were ranked. Factor in the weight for each rating. Job responsibility No. 1 carries more weight than 2, and so on.

(8) Ask for the employee's self assessment.

(9) Assess the total job, and select a tentative, overall rating.

(10) Match that rating against:
— the word description for that rating
— the employee's self rating
— your "G-Factor" rating

(11) Without disclosing your overall rating, ask colleagues or superiors to check your analysis and description of the employee's performance and to make their own evaluation. This provides a sounding-board against which to compare your findings.

(12) If discrepancies are found in (10) and (11), determine the reason. (For instance, was the assessment influenced by any of the *notions* in Chapter 1?). Then, either adjust your rating or prepare yourself better to support it.

(13) During the appraisal interview, discuss the *reasons* for the assessment with the employee.

Separate rating from coaching.

In summary, if rate you must, do so only at salary adjustment time. During other appraisal sessions, discuss *accomplishments* and *goals to be achieved* as a motivator to greater productivity. However you handle assessment, employees need to know, and, moreover, have a right to know. Responding to that need and right—communicating the assessment—is the topic of Section Three. It links *doing* the appraisal (Section Two) to *improving* the performance (Section Four).

APPLICATION AND REVIEW

1. Explain the difference between assessing performance and rating performance:

2. In your appraisals, how can you deal with problems raised by:
   (a) Task difficulty

   (b) Multiple contributions

   (c) Uncontrollable circumstances

   (d) Conflicting criteria

3. What is:
   (a) An inappropriate standard?

   (b) Task interdependence?

   (c) Task predictability?

   (d) Task visibility?

4. What are the four dimensions in the assessment pyramid?

5. What is the "G-factor?"

6. Note three ways you can make your assessments more reliable.
   (a)

   (b)

   (c)

SUGGESTED RESPONSES

1. Assessment is measuring performance against defined criteria (e.g., goals). A rating is a value, usually on a graded scale, assigned to the assessment.

3. (a) Refers to expectations that don't make sense—e.g., unrealistic goals.

    (b) Does the employee's success depend on others (e.g., a design engineer who must work closely with production personnel). The more interdependent the work is, the more difficult it is to assess.

    (c) The extent to which you can determine what to do and what will happen if you do it.

    (d) The degree to which you can observe an accomplishment, e.g., improving an employee's outlook, may go unnoticed, but a written report is seen by all.

4. The "G-factor" refers to the general leanings (preset attitudes and biases) of the assessor for or against employees that influence their ratings, regardless of the criteria or type of scale used.

5. Answers will vary.

SECTION THREE

COMMUNICATING
THE APPRAISAL

"You never told me my reports
were inadequate."

Where Section Two concentrated on the mechanics of PRD, this section features *communicating:* the human side of appraisals.

Chapter 8 defines communication, lists the reasons for discussing performance with employees, identifies the risks involved, and concludes with a 9-step strategy for conducting a PRD interview.

Chapter 9 exposes 30 traps managers can fall into when reviewing performance with employees.

The section concludes with a chapter on communication techniques for avoiding, neutralizing, or removing the traps, and ideas for enhancing the probability that appraisals will pay off in improved employee performance.

CHAPTER 8

A BLUEPRINT FOR COMMUNICATING THE APPRAISAL

"How come I'm being downgraded for a communications problem that was partly your fault?"

Notion 5 (In Chapter 1) hypothesized that communicating an assessment is more important than the assessment itself. Dialogue over the manner and conclusions of an appraisal starts the process of transferring a piece of paper into job action.

Communication is derived from the Latin *communis* or common. Bosses and subordinates operate in their own worlds, and little understanding occurs unless they develop a base for it (witness the quotation above).

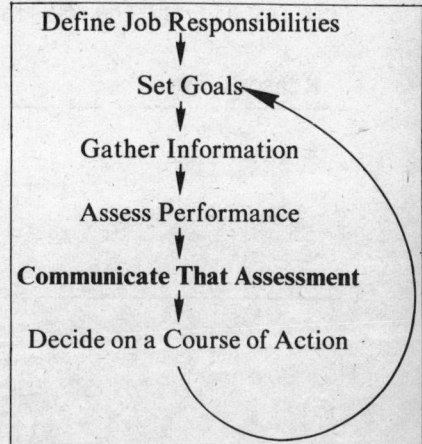

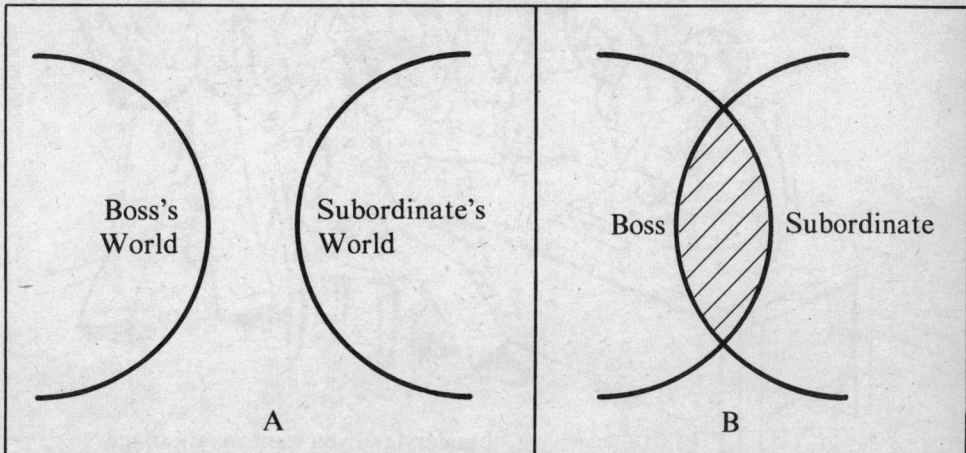

Define Job Responsibilities

Set Goals

Gather Information

Assess Performance

Communicate That Assessment

Decide on a Course of Action

Boss's World

Subordinate's World

A

Boss

Subordinate

B

Giving instruction (A in figure above) is not communicating; it's encoding: sending a message. Meaning is in the eyes of the receiver. It occurs when the message is decoded. Communication, then, is a two-way process, an interchange, a connection of experiences. Finding a common ground (B) from which to send and receive messages is the task of the communicator—in PRD, the appraiser.

Previous chapters stressed continuous and immediate feedback to employees concerning their performance. This chapter discusses why and constructs a framework for conducting a PRD interview. (The seminal ideas for this chapter were previously outlined in the author's *Managing The Interview,* John Wiley & Sons, Inc., 1981, Chapter 12.)

THE ADVANTAGES OF COMMUNICATING THE APPRAISAL

List the reasons why you should sit down with employees to discuss performance, and the risks inherent in this practice.

Reasons For	Risks

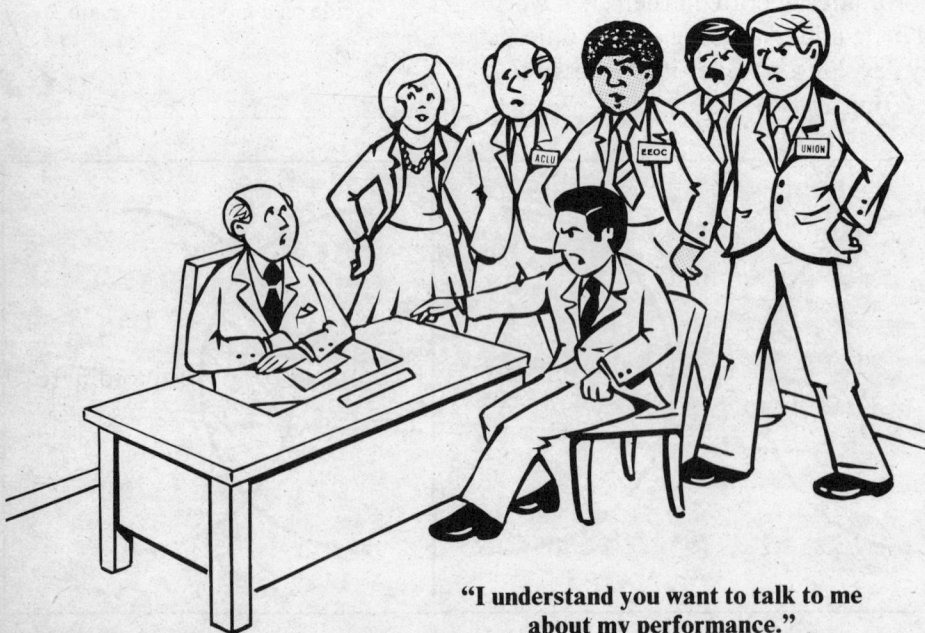

"I understand you want to talk to me about my performance."

The risks are aptly described in this monologue by an MPI manager:

"I don't feel comfortable going into this review. You know I don't understand everything about the job. What if I show my ignorance? There are
some things I feel but can't tell you why. You know, everything doesn't
have a reason for it. There are a couple of things I gotta tell MacCumhaill
that he's not going to like. He'll claim he's got too much paperwork to do
and not enough help. A lot of that's not under my control. And what if he
asks about salary or promotion? Everybody these days wants more money
and they want to move up the first six months on the job. That's not for me
to say, yet I'm expected to keep him motivated. And you just know he'll
ask me something I can't answer, or he'll disagree with my rating and start
comparing himself to others in the department. What'll I do then? I know
what he's been doing and I think I can point to a few areas where he can
improve. But I'm not sure how to improve them. You look at this whole
deal and I could be opening up a can of worms. Some things are better left
unsaid. If he goes away mad, then where am I? If that's what appraisal's
about, who needs it!"

Some of the MPI manager's concerns are real, some perceived. This entire
book is a response to them.

On the other side of the ledger, reviewing performance person-to-person
gives the manager and employee an opportunity to establish dialogue on
achievements during a given time-frame for the purpose of:

• Insuring that both agree on job requirements, expectations (goals),
  and priorities.
• Eliciting the employee's goals, motivations and aspirations.
• Checking the employee's self-assessment.
• Testing assumptions about each other and about the job, increasing
  the manager's credibility.
• Clarifying misunderstandings and avoiding future confusions.
• Evaluating the quality of performance by pinpointing areas in which
  the employee performed well and those in which minimum standards
  were not met.
• Sharing management's estimation of the performance.
• Strengthening the boss-subordinate relationship by establishing an
  atmosphere of fairness and trust.
• Spotting training needs.
• Developing a plan of action for improving the employee's performance
  and the boss's managing.

Whether conducting frequent mini-reviews or a once-(twice?)-a-year formal affair, managers can use the PRD interview as a self-corrector, a barom-
eter of things to come. Current problems can be dealt with, and future ones
anticipated.

STEPS IN COMMUNICATING PRD

1. **Preparation**
   Much of the preparation for a PRD interview was covered in Section Two, including:

   — Defining job responsibilities
   — Negotiating goals
   — Gathering and analyzing data
   — Completing the appraisal form
   — Soliciting the employee's self-evaluation
   — Reaching a tentative rating (if one is required), and testing it with superiors.

When appropriate, *arrange* a review with the employee. If this is a first session, ask the employee to examine the key elements of the appraisal form. If a veteran, ask him or her to think about one or two areas for development.

Schedule the PRD session to avoid interruptions such as phone calls and people walking into the room. Attempt to meet employees in as informal an atmosphere as possible, a neutral place such as a conference room. Allow ample time. Typically a formal session runs 1-3 hours.

Choose an appropriate time for the interview. Avoid pressure periods like the quarterly "pot-boiler," project or budget deadlines, etc. Neither the manager nor the employee should be hassled or emotionally involved in a current event. If so, better to postpone the review until a more relaxed time.

Develop an *interplan,* a design for interaction fitted to the employee's needs. Outline a sequence of topics to discuss, freely moving between goals and the employee's performance. Be prepared to vary the approach, depending on content emerging during the interview. The next page presents an interplan format, following the step-by-step schema in this chapter. Three columns provide space for listing topics the manager wants to cover, noting areas where more information is needed, and jotting down significant ideas emerging from the discussion.

INTERPLAN
(*PREPARATION* FOR CONDUCTING THE PRD INTERVIEW)

Name   Position

Steps in Communicating PRD	Topics to Cover	Areas to Probe	Notes on Responses
2. Warm-Up			
3. Job Responsibilities			
4. Performance Goals			
5. Job Accomplishments			
6. Areas for Improvement			
7. Rating			
8. Plan for Improvement			
9. Wrap-Up			

In preparing for the review, ask the following questions:

— Will what I am about to say *help*?
— What can I do to open communications?
— How can I control the situation in a non-defensive manner?
— How will it maintain or enhance the employee's esteem and self-image?
— What's the best way to ensure I accomplish my preset objectives?
— When the employee walks out of the room, what are the four or five questions I'd like to be able to answer about this person?

And finally, before going into the interview, *psych up,* or as one wit put it: "Take 30 seconds to meditate, just enough to clear your head for a minute."

2.   The Warm-Up

Anybody who has been through a performance review knows it's a nerve-racking business, especially for the person being appraised. In greeting the employee, establish a cordial, relaxed atmosphere.

Probably the best thing that can be said about "openers" is *be natural.* Subordinates immediately recognize a canned or phoney entrance. Start by talking about something that happened recently on the job that feel good about.

Early on, explain the objectives of the appraisal, assuring the employee of management's 100 percent backing and complete interest in his/her work.

Encourage the employee to talk first, defining the most important aspects of the job. Remember that both parties are there to *gain information* as well as to give it. Information gaps exist in any working relationship. Try to fill them.

3.   Job Responsibilities

Before discussing the person, discuss the job. Even though manager and employee have summarized the job before, the subordinate may still have different ideas about the exact nature of responsibilities. Ask before telling. Questions that can clarify differences are:

— Describe a typical day for me; what is it like?
— What is the major responsibility in your job, as you see it?
— Which tasks do you think are most important? Least important? Why?
— Which take the most time?
— What would you change?
— Do we agree on what your job is?
— Are there ways you think we could use your talents and your time more profitably?

4. Performance Goals

Briefly review the specific goals set for each job responsibility. Be sure the subordinate understands the standards by which performance is judged. Chapter 5 covered the topic of job responsibilities and goals.

5. Job Accomplishments

One common belief persists that employees tend to overrate themselves. Actually, employees are generally reluctant to say favorable things about themselves for fear of boasting. If the manager asks, "What do you think are your greatest strengths?" a little probing for "situations you feel good about" will frequently bring to the surface achievements that otherwise might go unnoticed. Two questions help to start the discussion:

— What has interested you most about the job in the last six months?
— In what areas do you feel you are becoming most effective?

The achievement need not be earthshaking. After listening to the employee's perception, add to the list from prior observations and analysis. Especially important are the favorable reactions of others to the employee's work.

6. Areas for Improvement

Sometimes this step is the most difficult part of a performance review. Most managers do not like giving negative information for fear of demotivating the employee or damaging future working relationships. (See Notion 1 in Chapter 1 and the guidelines for giving negative feedback in Chapter 10.) The questions below are helpful in stimulating discussion.

— What has disappointed you most about the job in the last year?
— In what areas do you feel least effective?
— What have you been doing to increase your effectiveness in these areas?
— What have I done to support and help you improve in these areas?
— What do I need to do to support and help you improve in these areas?

When employees have identified areas for improvement, the manager should add deficiencies from the PRD form. State these as positively as possible. Rather than badger and downgrade subordinates, speak of what needs to be done in the future. What has passed is past; they cannot change that. They *can* change tomorrow.

All areas for improvement need not be discussed in this interview. Emphasize the major ones and schedule other sessions as needed.

Chapter 6 emphasized the need for *specificity*. State improvement needs in concrete terms, so the employee can begin to *see* how to fulfill them.

7. The Rating

Communicate the overall rating if one is required (e.g., salary time), and as many of the specific ratings as necessary. Without accurately defining the status quo, there is no basis for developing future improvements. Cite specific examples to support the reasons for the employee's rating.

In cases where the rating has changed from the previous appraisal, the reasons for change, whether up or down, should be explained.

8. Plan of Development

PRD pays off mainly if a renewal program can be devised with the employee. A plan for improvement shifts the employee's thinking from unsatisfactory performance to: *Where do we go from here?*

In setting up a developmental plan, establish priorities. Begin with the most significant of the desired changes first: the changes that will result in a measurable improvement in performance. Concentrate your efforts and those of the employee on programs to enhance these areas. Recognize that it is not necessary to deal with every problem in one session. Experience shows that many interviews bog down when too much is covered at one time.

Once weaknesses have been recognized by subordinates, they will usually see the need for taking steps to eliminate them. However, they need help and support to set up specific plans and carry them out. Even if the employee cannot agree whole-heartedly with the manager's recommendations, some plan is better than none at all.

Set specific goals, with dates for starting and completion. Establish the mechanism for determining when each objective has been reached.

Do not wait for the next interview to think about how subordinates are progressing. Talk to them from time to time and indicate interest in their development, thus increasing the plan's chances for success. Remember that praise or criticism of performance is important at all times, not just during the interview. Immediacy and positiveness, rather than roar, count in feedback. Section Four details the particulars of improvement planning.

9. The Wrap-Up

- Ask the employee's reaction to the session and ways to improve it.
- Summarize the main points discussed. Go over the plan for improvement once again to be sure consensus has been reached on the proposed action steps.
- Set a date for the next review. Allow enough time to accomplish one or more of the improvement goals (30-90 days).

- Re-emphasize intentions to support and follow through on the improvement plan.
- Do not prolong the interview beyond this point. Once objectives have been accomplished, end the interview pleasantly.

These nine steps for communicating PRD are not meant to be lock-step procedures. They provide a guide that can be transposed into an interplan for making a positive impact on employees. The question is less whether the appraisal is negative or positive, but how it is handled and what has preceded it, its honesty, documented by legitimate observations, and its relevance to job performance.

Communicating PRD sometimes poses problems, succinctly summarized by our MPI manager. Dealing with these is the topic of the next two chapters.

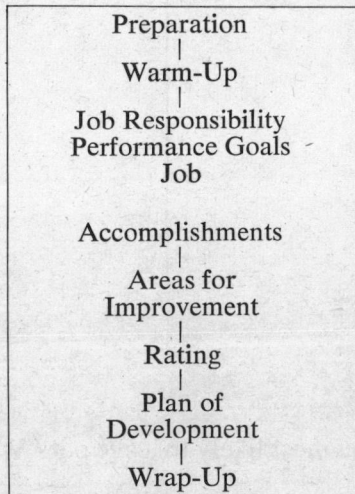

```
Preparation
    |
 Warm-Up
    |
Job Responsibility
Performance Goals
     Job

Accomplishments
    |
 Areas for
Improvement
    |
  Rating
    |
 Plan of
Development
    |
 Wrap-Up
```

APPLICATION AND REVIEW

1. A key to *communicating* is to:

2. In the left column, list the 9-step approach to communicating PRD.

    In the right column, note one thing you can do in your next appraisal to better implement each step.

    (a)

    (b)

    (c)

    (d)

    (e)

    (f)

    (g)

    (h)

    (i)

3. Which step(s) are you most likely to leave out? Which ones are most important to you?

4. Give at least 5 reasons why managers should discuss appraisals with their subordinates.

    (a)

    (b)

    (c)

    (d)

    (e)

SUGGESTED RESPONSES

1. Seek a common experience within which to interpret messages and find understanding.

2. Preparation, warm-up, job responsibilities, performance goals, job accomplishments, areas for improvement, the rating, plan of development, wrap-up.

3. Responses will vary.

4. Insure agreement on expectations, elicit employee goals and self assessment, pinpoint achievements and deficiencies, give management's assessment, strengthen relationships, test assumptions, clarify misunderstandings, spot training needs, develop improvement plans.

CHAPTER 9

TRAPS TO AVOID

"You say your door is always open, but have you ever tried to get by that secretary of yours?"

Although each employee is different and no two PRD interviews are the same, certain behaviors can turn any appraisal into disaster. This chapter presents an irreverent, tongue-in-cheek look at communication *traps*. (I could only think of 30. In a creative moment, you can add to the list.) Poor practices are exaggerated to show how they can ruin an otherwise well-prepared appraisal, where no review would have been better. (See also the author's "Blocks to Face-to-Face Communications" in *Management World,* January, 1975.)

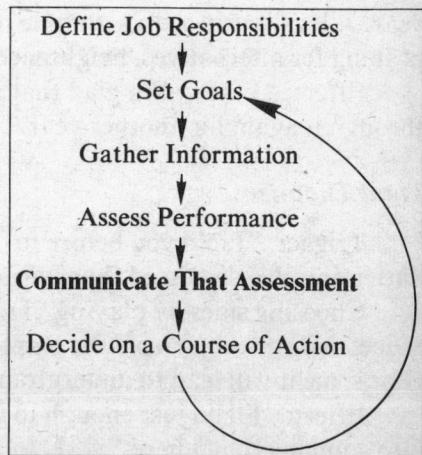

Define Job Responsibilities

Set Goals

Gather Information

Assess Performance

Communicate That Assessment

Decide on a Course of Action

Off-the-Cuff Delivery

Trigger: "I know there's an appraisal form around here someplace. I saw it on my desk a couple of weeks ago. Well now, we'll just have to proceed without it."

Spur of the moment appraisals, without preparation, insure that inconsequential topics are covered and momentous ones left out. After all, you're only dealing with the employee's career (and yours, for that matter). Spend your time on "more important things."

Effect: "Nobody cares."

The Surprise Party

Trigger: "Guess what, Adams. I've been keeping book on you for the last six months. I got a list here a mile long I want to go over with you. Do you remember back in June when . . ."

Now everybody likes surprises. Letting your assessment slip out during the year will take the sting out of the December session. Play it close to the vest.

Effect: "This appraisal's unfair. This guy is out to hang me."

The Pressure Cooker

Trigger: "We're here to see if you cut the mustard, Hendricks. But I have to conclude this in a hurry. I only have 15 minutes before a big meeting with the VP."

Create a *guillotine* atmosphere by keeping employees hanging in the balance and making them feel responsible for taking up your valuable time. Pressure moments are easy to generate. Let the employee wait, look at your watch a lot, mention how busy you are, or talk about the exploits of other employees. Right up front, hit the employee with negatives and mistakes made during the year. A let's-get-it-over-with tone makes for more talking, less listening and probing for alternatives, heightened frustration, and missed information.

Effect: "Whew, I'm glad that's over. Thank goodness I don't have to go through it again for another year."

I and Thou-ism

Trigger: "I told you before to correct that situation. You know what your duties are. I've discussed them with you a thousand times."

Choosing sides by playing "I vs. you" leads to defensiveness and resistance, and should turn off the employee for the remainder of the interview. (For some it will lead to underground resistance.)

Effect: "I'll do just enough to get by and that's it. I wonder how you look into a union around here."

The Preacher

Trigger: "If you could only understand what I'm trying to tell you. Now let me tell you how I used to do it when I was a supervisor. Then you can follow that example."

This trap has three parts to it:

1) Conduct sermons on the goodness of working hard.
2) Talk down to employees like parent to child: "You know, Barbara, you shouldn't have spoken to Mr. Henderson that way." This should create a proper air of guilt and inferiority.
3) Convert them to your way of thinking. Since conversion is a form of slavery, if you want employees to do what they're told, preach hellfire and brimstone.

Effect: "Ho-hum, there he goes again," or "I'm sorry, I feel so bad."

The Defender

Trigger: "What do you mean, we make too many changes in the schedule!"

Since tightroping through the interview is desirable, prepare your defenses ahead of time. Remember: a strong defense neutralizes the opponent's offense. To keep the employee off balance, use such devises as raising your voice when your logic is weak, to convey certainty.

Effect: "You can't criticize a single thing around here. I'm not going to say anything next time."

The Warrior

Trigger: "From the very beginning, I knew your way wouldn't succeed."

Think of the performance appraisal interview as a small war where you win and the subordinate loses. Of course, you may have to rig events in your favor, because the subordinate probably wants to win too. This competitive approach leads from nowheresville to antagonism, but you keep the subordinate on guard.

Effect: "I'll get even."

The Mime

Trigger: "You're the cause of our problems on the line."

You need not say this, of course, because just pointing your finger, scrunching up your face, and scowling will convey the same message. Miming is energy-conserving. Yawning, clipping your fingernails, fixing your eyes to a spot on the wall, shaking your head — all such behaviors transmit messages to employees, putting them in their proper place.

Effect: "Your non-verbal behavior is making so much noise I can't hear what you're saying!"

The Past-Dweller

Trigger: "It's the same dumb thing you did two years ago."

Keeping the spotlight on historic events precludes the need to propose future solutions.

Effect: "Make one mistake and they never forget. What about all my successes?"

The Stickler

Trigger: "The truth of the matter is that you've been making 6.1 calls per day, not 7.2."

Bosses are synonymous with wisdom. Since you're in the best position to interpret happenings, stick to your facts. Naturally, subordinates distort data to place themselves in a good light.

Effect: "You never look at my side of it."

Playing God

Trigger: "Miss Huebner, send MacCumhaill in now. I'm ready for him."

It helps if you sit in an oversized executive chair, raised so that you loom above the subordinate. One well-known admiral was said to have shortened by two inches the front legs of the interviewee's chair, placing him in an uneasy, subservient position. You can add to this feeling by looking *down* over your glasses and vast desk at the lowly subordinate. Playing God should produce disciples who will follow you anywhere, even across the stormy seas of reduced sales or slowdowns in production.

Effect: "Oh, God."

The Little Professor

Trigger: "Now listen carefully. I'm going to tell you exactly how to do it."

You set this trap by pontificating on your experience and know-how. Conduct the appraisal like a classroom, so that employees can learn from it. The formula is: lecture, ask a question (to insure they're still awake), lecture some more.

Effect: "She must think I'm a nitwit and have no ideas of my own. After all, I've only done the job a hundred times before."

The Lover

Trigger: "I suppose, Harry, I really can't hold you responsible for not making sales. I'm sure that there were extenuating circumstances."

Conduct appraisals to win the employee's affection and devotion, even at the expense of accepting inferior work. Take care not to hurt the employee's feelings or ruffle any feathers.

Effect: "Boy, is he a pushover."

The Deaf Ear

Trigger: "Sure, sure, whatever you think. Excuse me, I've gotta take this important call."

Listening takes valuable time away from other duties. Make up your mind first, then there's no need to lend an ear (you'll need it when the EEOC investigator comes around). One way to turn a deaf ear is to interrupt. Since you've already decided on the rating, there's no logical reason to allow employees to launch diatribes. Cut them off and save yourself a migraine.

Effect, "Well, I tried to tell him but nobody around here seems to care."

The One-Way Street

Trigger: "Surely you wouldn't be so dumb as to do it that way, would you?"

Make statements and ask questions that leave little room for an answer, or, at best, a binary response (yes or no). Painting dead-end signs is akin to building one-way streets, so eventually there's nowhere to go.

Effect: "You can't win around here."

Righteousness

Trigger: "I may not be right, but I'm never wrong." (A pronouncement by one of my professors in undergraduate days.)

Insist on always being right, lest you lose your authority and respect. And besides, what do employees know?

Effect: "Uhmmm, that arrogant, no good SOB."

Type Casting

Trigger: "Those people in production never plan ahead. All they do is go from day to day."

It saves a lot of time and energy if you can catalog things and people into neat niches. It will also relieve you and the employee from having to think.

Effect: "Some of my best friends are production people."

Broad Jumping

Trigger: "Obviously, Mumford, you're not giving the job your all. That's why the project wasn't in on time."

The technique is to jump from very little data to sweeping generalizations. This trap can be sprung while doing the appraisal, and finished when communicating it. Don't let the facts get in the way; it's better to put your foot in your mouth than in the employee's backside. Another form of broadjumping is to assume agreement. For instance, preface every conclusion with, "Of course, you agree that . . ." If employees say "yes," nod their heads or do nothing, that means they are in agreement. Subordinates are by nature shy, so unless they explode vociferously or pound fists on your walnut desk, assume mutual understanding. What they do after they walk out the door is of no concern to you.

Effect: "I quit!"

Obfuscation

Trigger: "Improve your interface with others, making it possible for them to interact meaningfully with you."

Avoid clarifying reasons for your assessment, and studiously avoid suggestions for solving problems. Choose your words like slippery eels. Shuffle papers and build castles in the air.

Effect: "What did he say? What did he say?"

Name-Calling

Trigger: "Elizabeth, why are you so unlikeable?"

Core the employee's personality by calling her rigid, lazy, hostile, and suspicious. Name-calling keeps the employee on the defensive so she can't ask embarrassing questions.

Effect: "He doesn't like me."

Generalizing

Trigger: "That's the way we've always done it, and you know I only have the best interests of your career in mind."

Keep your analysis at such a general level that it's difficult not to agree. It's hard to take issue with an abstraction. Specifying rhyme or reason can only get you in trouble.

Effect: "I'm exhausted. We talked for an hour and I'm more confused now than when I went in for my appraisal."

Passing the Buck

Trigger: "Well, I agree with you but, you know, the people up there make the policies, and what can I do?"

When in doubt, cast aspersions on others, especially gesticulating upward toward the executive suite. Blaming higher authority gets you off the hook and lets employees know that everyone is equally helpless: "We're all on the Titanic together."

Effect: "With management like that, I wonder how in the world this company makes money."

Information Overload

Trigger: "I have three reports that may be of interest here. Why don't I read them?"

Talk about a problem long enough, and people may think you've solved it. If you talk a lot, employees won't get a chance to disagree with you. Inundate them with information, and the response will be to label, box and bury.

Effect: "I give up."

The Inquisition

Trigger: "Why's your scrappage up 1/10 of 1 percent? Why did you let that grievance get out of hand? Why aren't you motivating your employees?

How come your absenteeism rate is the highest in the division?"

Machine gun questions from all sides, until the employee is forced to take cover. This third degree approach should allow you to be in complete command at all times.

Effect: (silence)

Recycling

Trigger: "As I said before . . ."

Like pipe smoke, let the conversation drift in lazy circles. Circumvent the real issues by leading employees around and repeating yourself a lot, without reaching an explanation or end point. Do this until employees shrug their shoulders and accept your assessment. An added attraction of this trap: Recycling is in.

Effect: "Do we have to go over this again? I've heard it all before."

Hidden Agendas

Trigger: "Are you happy here, Ludwith?"

Hide at least one agenda item during each appraisal interview, e.g., *I'm gonna let 'em know who's boss today,* or *I gotta get this over with in a hurry so I can get to my golf date,* or *I gotta force Ludwith to resign somehow.* Hidden agendas provide mystery and ambiguity to the appraisal. They're puzzles for subordinates to solve. If they know your every thought, they won't be bedazzled by your profundity. Operating with hidden agendas lends a mystique, a new depth to your analyses.

Effect: "What's she getting at?"

Face-Saving

Trigger: "I'll make that decision, Carsten, because you've got this project all fouled up."

The best way to save face is to make the other person lose his. A major aim of the appraisal interview is to make sure that Carsten gets put in his place at least once a year. Causing subordinates to lose face from time to time will inhibit complacency.

Effect: "That SOB. I hate him."

The Praise Up-Shoot Down Sandwich

Trigger: "Your people seem to have better morale, Hopkins, since you implemented that suggestion program (pause) . . . *however,* you've fallen behind in filling your orders (pause) . . . but I am glad to see your employees happier."

This trap is set by complimenting, criticizing, then complimenting again. Sandwiching the negatives make them unnoticeable, and prevents employees from getting too upset. With this technique, they ought to be able to stomach three or four sandwiches in one sitting.

Effect: "I must be doing a pretty good job. He hardly criticized my work at all."

Put it in Writing

Trigger: "If you don't agree with my proposal, Aubrey, why don't you write up your plan and submit it in triplicate on Form SPC-016782."

That should stop most of your subordinates. Just in case a couple persist, correct their documents and send them back for resubmission.

Effect: "Paperwork, paperwork, paperwork. That's all I need — another form to fill out."

Promissory Notes

Trigger: "Oh sure, I'll take care of that."

If by chance the first 29 traps don't get them, this one is guaranteed to be a sure-fire success. Make commitments if you must, but forget them once the appraisal interview is over. Follow-through creates more work that really isn't necessary. Employees should know what is expected. If not, tell them exactly what to do by memo.

Effect: "Promises, promises, promises!"

The point is made. It's not difficult to botch up a performance appraisal. Like a minefield, traps are all around, and, despite the best of intentions, even the most practiced managers occasionally fall into them. The responsibility of appraisers is to know where explosive problems exist and avoid, remove, or neutralize them. But first, we must sense traps exist. Awareness is at least half of the coping. Once aware, we can take remedial action. Those actions are the content of the next chapter.

APPLICATION AND REVIEW

1.   In the left column are the communication traps discussed in this chapter. On the right, state how you can avoid, remove, or neutralize them in your next appraisal review.

Traps	Avoidance, Neutralization, or Removal Strategy
Off-the-Cuff Delivery	
The Surprise Party	
The Pressure Cooker	
I and Thou-ism	
The Preacher	
The Defender	
The Warrior	
The Mime	
The Past Dweller	
The Stickler	
Playing God	
The Little Professor	
The Lover	
The Deaf Ear	
The One-Way Street	
Righteousness	
Type Casting	
Broad Jumping	
Obfuscation	
Name-Calling	
Generalizing	
Passing the Buck	
Information Overload	
The Inquisition	
Recycling	

Traps	Avoidance, Neutralization, or Removal Strategy
Hidden Agendas	
Face Saving	
The Praise Up-Shoot Down Sandwich	
Put it in Writing	
Promissory Notes	

CHAPTER 10

SUGGESTIONS FOR IMPROVING THE APPRAISAL INTERVIEW

"You tell me what to do, but I can't tell you anything!"

In previous chapters we discussed the importance of being specific, of communicating regularly and systematically, of preparing, of clarifying responsibilities and goals, of scheduling an appropriate time and place for discussing the review, and of establishing two-way communications. This chapter presents a bouillabaisse of ideas and techniques for communicating the appraisal, but not all suggestions apply to your situation; pick and choose the ones that are appropriate and appear feasible in your work environment.

Define Job Responsibilities
↓
Set Goals
↓
Gather Information
↓
Assess Performance
↓
Communicate that Assessment
↓
Decide on a Course of Action

Fine-Tune Your Radar. Be aware of and keep alert to the notions discussed in Chapter 1 and the pitfalls described in Chapter 9. Some of these can be overcome in preparation, and others as they occur during the interview. Sensing and removing traps may not, of itself, improve communications, but it paves the way for open and honest dialogue.

Ask Open Questions. If our aim is to open up discussions, avoid asking binary, global, threatening, and cued questions. If a question can be answered "yes" or "no" (*binary*), it is probably a poor question. A *global* question is usually too general for an employee to get a handle on it, e.g., "Tell me about the year; what's your assessment of it?" *Threatening* questions like "Why in the world didn't you meet that deadline?" and *cued* questions—ones with the answers included, e.g.; "You couldn't possibly consider that a good approach, could you?"—tend to induce caution and defensiveness.

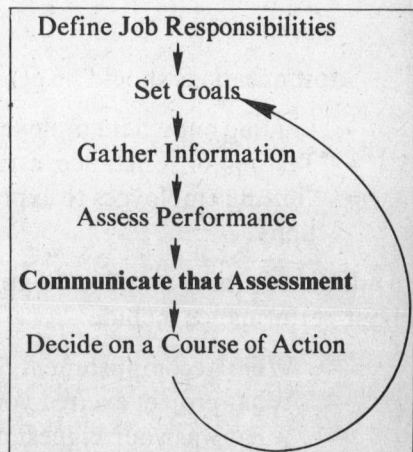

> Jack R. Gibb, in the *Journal of Communication,*
> (Volume 11, September, 1961, pp. 141–148.) defines defen-
> siveness as behavior that occurs when individuals perceive or
> anticipate threat. They devote considerable energy to defend-
> ing their position, to devising ways to be seen more favorably,
> to winning, dominating, or escaping the perceived or antici-
> pated attack. Defensiveness prevents listeners from accurately
> perceiving the intentions of the communicator. It distorts
> meaning. In short, defensive behavior produces defensive lis-
> tening.
>
> The reverse is also in effect. That is, as defenses are re-
> duced, listeners are better able to concentrate on the content of
> the communication.

Most questions should be geared to:

- Finding out what employees think, what they like and dislike.
- Testing for resistance, attitudes, opinions, and controversy.
- Getting employees to express their frustrations as well as their aspira-
tions.

In addition to those noted in Chapter 8, some questions to stimulate discussion
about performance include:

— What accomplishment do you feel best about?
— What project excited you most?
— What was your biggest disappointment in the job?
— What current project is most challenging to you?
— Which is most boring?
— If you could wave a wand, what would you be doing five years from
now?
— How would you change the job to produce more effective results?
— How would you change the department to obtain more effective
results?
— How would you change the organization to gain more effective
results?
— What are the key behaviors that lead to success in this job?
— Which ones would lead to failure?
— With whom do you interact most frequently on the job?
— With whom would you like to have more interaction (input, cooper-
ation) on the job?
— What do you feel are your major assets?

— What one area would you like most to develop over the next six months?

Other questions to draw out more information:

— Why did it turn out that way?
— Why do production (marketing, finance, etc.) react the way they do?
— Why do employees quit early?
— Why do you feel that way?
— Why was that project so satisfying to you?
— Why were you disappointed? Elated?
— If you had to pinpoint one cause of the problem, what would it be?
— Do you have other reasons for feeling as you do?
— I hadn't thought of that; how would you carry it out?
— I'm not sure I understand that; could you expand on it?
— What do you think? What is your reaction to that?

Listen. The effectiveness of a PRD interview increases with your understanding of a subordinate's point of view. If you interrupt and dominate the conversation, you may miss an opportunity to find out what motivates your employee.

Listening is a much talked about, but little practiced management skill. There are at least four levels of listening for understanding. The appraiser may:

(a) Remain silent, ignoring what the other person is saying and thinking about the next question or comment.
(b) Pay attention, but give no indication of hearing.
(c) Paraphrase key ideas of the employee to check for misunderstandings and encourage development of further ideas.
(d) Probe for the causes and feelings behind what is stated. If strong feelings are present, put them into words. For instance, "You sound anxious about this situation," or "You seem bitter about this," or "That gives you a real sense of achievement."

The more accurately you *hear* what subordinates say, the better your chance to help them perform more effectively.

React Out of the Context of the Review. Build on information, verbal and nonverbal, presented by the employee. One technique is to literally stop to ask yourself: "What's going on?" "What am I reacting to?" "What am I feeling right now?" "Why am I reacting or feeling this way?" Answering these questions can help clarify and weigh responses and redirect probes for information. Pauses, too, can produce unsolicited information from employees that would not otherwise be revealed.

One reaction that can stimulate two-way communication is to empathize with the employee: "Yes, I understand what that's like." This does not mean agreement or disagreement, but gives a feeling of acceptance and encouragement to participate fully in the appraisal.

Search for Intentions. No formal PRD interview should take place without a prior meeting with the employee. In that preliminary session, search out information gaps that will increase the accuracy of the assessment. Search for intentions behind the behavior and meaning between the lines. Become sensitive to such nonverbal behaviors as hesitation, a frown, a smile, excited tone of voice, signs of anger, frustration, pleasure, or apathy. Eye contact is frequently a measure of ease and confidence in the employee. (See Chapter 12 for a discussion of the relationship between intentions, actions, and effects.)

Speak of "We." Talk in terms of "we" rather than "I." "*We*'ve discussed this a number of times; how do you think *we* can improve it?" This is more than a communication trick. It signifies a willingness to share responsibility for unacceptable performance. It suggests that the manager and employee are together. In interdependency there is strength.

Change Places with the Employee. Try on, figuratively, the employee's shoes. Mentally transpose yourself—you sit in the appraisee's chair. How would you like the session to be conducted? What concerns do you have? This mental inversion can provide the *common* experience, discussed in Chapter 8, from which to launch the appraisal discussion.

Spotlight the Job. Focus on responsibilities and goals rather than character traits. Three suggestions:

(a) Avoid attributing poor performance to characteristics of the employee: e.g., rigidity, bad attitude, disloyalty. Instead analyze the job and ways to work more effectively.

(b) Try to describe performance without interpreting it: e.g., "Three deadlines were not met in the first quarter," vs. "you're disorganized and you procrastinate too much."

(c) Avoid generalities and clichés. Misunderstanding often occurs when two people interpret a word or phrase differently. You can circumvent this problem by clearly defining important words in job terms, and asking the employee to do the same. Avoid such comments as:
— "There's one thing you have to understand . . ."
— "Let sleeping dogs lie."
— "That's obvious."
— "No one else in the department has that problem."
— "We've always done it that way."
— "I told you so."
— "It'll pass."
— "That's the way the cookie crumbles."
— "You've got a communications problem."

Feedback Negatives. Except in heated moments, most of us hesitate to give negative feedback. Some guidelines for discussing deficient performance are:

(a)   Target one negative at a time. Don't overload employees so that they feel inadequate.

(b)   State the negative in terms of the job, rather than the employee. For instance, describe a job that was not accomplished rather than the accusation: "Why are you so lazy?"

(c)   Check employees' perception of the problem.

(d)   Express understanding. This doesn't mean agreement with employee perceptions, but you at least can see "where they are coming from."

(e)   Discuss possible causes. Probe employees' views. If they rationalize or point the finger at outside sources, point out factors that are in their control.

(f)   Agree on remedial actions. Together, work out a solution that employees will commit themselves to and, from your vantage, will get the job done.

(g)   Share responsibility for translating the negative into a positive. It is difficult to turn performance around without the manager's encouragement. Commit to some specific action in support of employees. Talk in terms of the *we-ness* mentioned earlier.

(h)   End on a positive note. Criticism is difficult for anyone. Make sure the session doesn't conclude on a downer. Don't linger on the past that cannot be undone. Focus on future corrective action and benefits.

Follow Through. To insure that the review produces results, record your impressions and suggestions for improvement. Make sure both agree on what to do to improve. Set deadlines for accomplishing the improvement and for meeting again to discuss progress and potential problems. Whatever you commit to, make sure you deliver (see Chapter 12 on planning for improvement). Talk *is* cheap. Go where the action is. *Do more, talk less.*

Deal with Disagreement. Prepare for some disagreement in discussing performance. After all, managers and employees view the same job from varying positions in the company. A different set of facts are known to each. Absolute agreement may be unattainable, although mutual understanding on basic points should be reached.

When disagreement occurs, bear these points in mind:

(a)   Listen to the employee. Usually when bosses are challenged, they tend to come on strong and do very little listening. The objective is to hear another point of view. This gives you a chance to evaluate the reasonableness of the employee's position and reconcile it with your own.

(b)   Restate the employee's opinion (see "Listen" on page 141).

(c)   Confirm your understanding of the employee's position. Do this with direct questions: "Have I stated your main ideas correctly?"

(d)   Pinpoint reasons for disagreement. Do not argue or defend. Make an attempt to determine if the subordinate's contentions are sound. Is the disagreement factual? Is additional reassurance necessary in order to avoid an emotional discussion?

(e)   Discuss ways to resolve problems. Ask for the employee's ideas, then state yours.

(f)   Negotiate a resolution. If the discussion has been positive and non-argumentative, with an honest effort to get at cause and effect, then you have the basis for resolution.

(g)   Be open to new data that will alter the situation. This openness refers to you and the employee. Just the act of committing to openness may be enough to lead to resolution. Rather than diminish the employee, aim to resolve the disagreement and increase production. This requires a receptive attitude on both sides.

(h)   If no agreement is reached, reschedule another session in a few days. *Mull* time is helpful. After further reflection, the employee may change, or you may change your stand.

Deal with Apathy. Occasionally an employee will be indifferent to the appraisal. The question is *why*. Determine if something in the interview triggered the behavior. If you feel the employee is threatened by the assessment process, go over the objectives of PRD and the need for open, honest dialogue on performance. Ask a question about a known interest or accomplishment and build on it. Induce the employee to talk by asking for an opinion and following up with "why" and "how" questions.

Another kind of apathy is over-agreement—employees who say "yes" to everything to avoid unpleasantness, yet have no intention of changing their behavior. Under these circumstances, make certain they understand the improvement needed, get them to indicate how they intend to fulfill the expectation, agree on a written plan of action with a schedule for reviewing progress, and finally, insist that they summarize the evaluation in their terms.

Deal with Emotions. On a rare occasion, employees may get angry when you point out weaknesses in their performance, regardless of how tactfully you criticize. Don't make things worse by losing your temper. Instead, let them talk, and listen patiently. If the emotional level remains intense, reschedule the review. Try to calm employees by explaining that your purpose is to give them another opportunity to talk after having had a few days to think things over. Do not let them leave while still upset. Begin the second interview by discussing why the first one became so emotional. If an employee appears excessively anxious (there is always some tension at the beginning of the interview), offer reassurance that the review is not an inquisition, emphasize the positive values of PRD to employees and to the organization, and initiate an immediate discussion of one of the employee's achievements. (That is unless, of course, you mean it to be an inquisition. Then the session becomes more a disciplinary review than an appraisal.)

Deal with Impatience. Some employees, particularly younger ones, may not be realistic in their expectations for raises, promotions or transfers. Normally, raises and promotions should not be discussed in a PRD session focused on improving performance, but sometimes it cannot be avoided. Where employees react to a favorable evaluation by asking for an immediate tangible reward, you might try these approaches:

(a)   Explain that successful performance *over a period of time* is required to justify an increase or promotion.

(b)   Remind them that others are qualified and must be considered for available openings.

(c)   Assure them that they will be considered along with others for future opportunities, provided their work continues to be excellent. Suggest steps they can take to prepare for a better position.

(d)   Do not make any promises, because all decisions depend on their future development and the availability of openings.

Where employees expect a raise or promotion despite poor performance and potential, your job is to point out where their performance is lacking. They may not accept it, but at least your assessment is known. Better that than letting pressure build to a major explosion later on.

Deal with the Individual Who Wants to Resign. On occasion, employees may threaten to resign. If their performance has been good and you believe they have a future, attempt to determine the basis for the decision. Ask them if your evaluation contributed to the decision (it's unlikely that this would be the sole reason). By encouraging them to talk, you may discover clues to the true causes of dissatisfaction. If the reason for leaving is greater compensation or responsibility with another organization, emphasize opportunities for future growth, and weigh giving up a better long-term situation for a temporary advantage. If the reason for leaving has resulted from some misunderstanding, set the record straight. Encourage them to wait 30 days (or some other period of time) before making a final decision, and invite them to discuss the matter with the appropriate executive.

Experiment with Alternative Techniques. Try something different in each PRD interview; habits smother new approaches. This does not mean viable techniques should be abandoned, but rather that you should deliberately set out to add additional skills. For example:

•   Conduct a PRD interview where the employee does 90 percent of the talking.

•   Hold the interview in a non-office/desk setting.

- Ask subordinates to assess themselves.
- Meet with a subordinate for half an hour per month in a mini-assessment session.
- Devise a notation system for keeping a running account of an employee's performance.

Exchange ideas and problems with other appraisers. Discuss PRD interviews with colleagues. Find out how other managers handle difficult appraisal situations.

End the PRD Interview on a High. Build an image of potential rather than an image of doom (unless, of course, you plan to fire the subordinate). Improved job performance, not punishment, is your aim.

Evaluate Your Appraisal Practices. Any management function must be reflected on periodically if you are to determine its effectiveness. A critical part of face-to-face interactions with subordinates is evaluating your own performance.

The PRD interview is an awesome responsibility, and frequently has long-term implications for subordinates and for the company. Managers should continually ask: "Is it accomplishing what I hoped it would?" One criterion for judging the PRD interview is: does the employee walk out saying, "I may not get the exact raise I want or be promoted tomorrow, but at least I had an opportunity to present myself."

Here are some questions to ask yourself immediately after you conduct your next appraisal interview:

— How comfortable do I feel with the review?
— Did I establish two-way communication?
— What do I feel uneasy about?
— How satisfied is the subordinate?
— How do I feel toward the subordinate?
— How receptive was the subordinate to my suggestions?
— Did I sense any points of disagreement? If so, which ones?
— Did I avoid getting into personality traits?
— What subject aroused interest and involvement?
— What information gaps exist that I need to fill?
— What parts of the appraisal did I feel most comfortable with? Least comfortable with?
— What traps did I fall into?
— What will I do differently in the next PRD interview?
— What further information do I need?
— What specific commitments were made as a result of the review?
— What do I need to do over the next three months to support the subordinate's effort?
— Why did the subordinate react the way he or she did?
— What skills do I need to develop and sharpen?

— What effect will the PRD interview have on the subordinate's performance over the next three months?

The suggestions in this chapter are not all inclusive, but they represent a starting point. Usually they will contribute to improved appraisals. On occasion, though, you may be confronted with an employee who is not performing, after repeated efforts to correct the situation. The frustration of continuing such an antagonistic relation hurts you and the organization. At this point, you should seriously consider termination.

But keep in mind: most problems with difficult employees can be prevented by setting clear goals in advance, by refusing to get entangled in personality clashes and by involving employees in their own efforts. This involvement, and its link to increased productivity are addressed in the final section of the book.

APPLICATION AND REVIEW

1. Experiment: List 5 approaches or techniques you have not tried that you can use in your next PRD interview:

   (a)

   (b)

   (c)

   (d)

   (e)

2. Identify 8 guidelines for giving negative feedback:

   (a)

   (b)

   (c)

   (d)

   (e)

   (f)

   (g)

   (h)

3. List the guidelines for dealing with disagreement:

   (a)

   (b)

   (c)

   (d)

   (e)

   (f)

   (g)

   (h)

SUGGESTED RESPONSES

1.   Responses will vary.

2.   Target one negative
     State in job terms
     Check the employee's perception
     Express understanding
     Discuss causes
     Agree on a remedy
     Share responsibility
     End on a positive note

3.   Listen
     Restate the employee's position
     Confirm your understanding
     Pinpoint reasons for disagreement
     Discuss solutions
     Negotiate resolution
     Be open to change views
     (Reschedule, if no agreement)

Now, does anyone else want to question his performance appraisal?

SECTION FOUR

APPRAISALS FOR GREATER INVOLVEMENT AND PRODUCTIVITY

This final section focuses on the ultimate thrust of appraisals — to improve performance and increase productivity. Two major topics are treated:

- Involving subordinates in PRD
- Planning for improvement

Chapter 11 presents a 6-dimensional model for measuring how effectively you include subordinates in the appraisal process. A case for greater involvement is developed, risks and conditions are accounted for, kinds of participation are defined, and six guidelines are drafted for encouraging and managing employee involvement.

The last chapter emphasizes how appraisals are implemented, the benefits of developing an action plan, and six guidelines for translating appraisals into improved performance, and, ultimately, greater productivity.

CHAPTER 11

INVOLVING EMPLOYEES IN THEIR APPRAISALS

"If I cannot influence the gods
I shall set all hell in motion."

Vergil's *The Aeneid*

Two worldwide trends over the last generation seem persistent: the demand of individuals to control their own lives and the escalation of the war for human rights. Their impact is obvious in national and international affairs. They have had their affect on organizations as well. The involvement of subordinates in decision making has been bantered back and forth in management circles for most of the century, stirring many unanswered questions:

Does employee participation make for higher morale?
Do managers have time to involve subordinates?
What happens to efficiency when others "get in the act"?
Will managers face problems they can't handle as a result of involvement?
What is the relationship between involvement and productivity?
Do managers relinquish authority by involving subordinates?
Do managers give up influence?

These legitimate questions have not been conclusively answered by practitioners nor researchers.

Standard textbooks talk about direction and control. This chapter emphasizes involvement and autonomy. The history of so-called *democratic* management is replete with derogatory terms like "behavior scientism," soft-headedness," "Mr. Milktoast," "a Walter Mitty." A great philosopher of the 20th century, John Dewey, was denigrated for advocating the involvement of students in their own learning. His critics called it *permissive* education— "let the kid chop down the piano to find out what the music is like." They totally misconstrued Dewey's position, which insisted that every idea be tested against experience and reconstructed according to the results. His concept of education demanded the highest order of social and intellectual activity. Yet, because he advocated the involvement of the students (subordinates), he was labeled a namby-pamby, do-as-you-please theorist.

Involvement, as discussed in this chapter, has nothing to do with the soft/hard, lenient/tough dichotomies. It places greater demands on employees as well as managers. At times, managers need to act unilaterally; there are decisions that they and only they can make. But, since appraisal is a continuing, thought-through process, it offers a greater opportunity than most situations to include employees.

Below are 15 pairs of statements. Each pair is assigned 10 points. Allocate the 10 points to each statement, according to the extent with which you agree. For instance, if you totally agree with 1A, you would score it 10 and give a zero to 1B. If your agreement is less than total, you might score 7(1A) and 3(1B). If both statements make equal sense to you, assign 5 points to each.

_____ 1A.   Employees should resent tasks and goals imposed from the top, with little regard for feedback.

_____ 1B.   Managers need to be leaders, especially when it comes to communicating tasks and goals. They need the courage to be unpopular.

_____ 2A.   Employees cannot be expected to be objective or impartial enough to put managerial goals first in matters of conflict.

_____ 2B.   Managers can't really be expected to put consideration of the workers higher on the priority scale than production goals.

_____ 3A.   When talking to subordinates, calling a spade a spade often takes courage that proves the true mettle of managers.

_____ 3B.   It's often more intelligent to soften an evaluation and take a political or tactful approach in dealing with personnel problems.

_____ 4A.   Employee morale is vital to productivity in the long run, and should not be disturbed for some short-term gain.

_____ 4B.   Managers need to have vision for the possible and must be objective about tasks, even if short-term morale problems are the result.

_____ 5A.   Employees should be involved in the screening process leading to the hiring of *managers*.

_____ 5B.   Managers know the needs of management and are quite capable of hiring supervisory personnel.

_____ 6A.   With their superior training and overview, managers know what is going on more than employees.

_____ 6B.   The collective judgment of a work team about the job is more accurate than the opinion of one supervisor.

_____ 7A.   Employees should have the freedom to experiment, even if short-term productivity is lessened or mistakes are made.

_____ 7B.   Managers should not allow employee freedom to occur at the expense of productivity.

_____ 8A.   Management must absolutely retain control over allocation of resources.

_____ 8B.   Allocation of resources in budgets should happen after consultation with employees.

_____ 9A.   Employees cannot be expected to be stern with their own colleagues on matters of non-compliance with regulations.

_____ 9B.   The disciplining of errant employees can often be left to other employees.

_____ 10A.   Employees and managers need to be close, including the formation of friendships and shared social interactions.

_____ 10B.   Managers need to be aloof from employees in order to be good leaders; togetherness reduces strictness and discipline.

_____ 11A.   Employees should be included in most management committees, ad hoc or permanent, in order to insure full scope considerations.

_____ 11B.   The presence of employees in managerial committees inhibits objectivity and efficient consideration of managerial goals.

_____ 12A.   Managers must insist on the right to establish output levels of production.

_____ 12B.   Because employees know and understand their own skills and the tools they use, they can best establish realistic output levels of production.

_____ 13A.   Managers would be naive if they were to rely exclusively on employee honesty in evaluation processes.

_____ 13B.   Employees are essentially honest about their strengths and shortcomings, and their self evaluations can be expected to be relatively accurate.

_____ 14A.   Managers need to assert leadership in hiring employees. There is no way they can honestly pass the buck to employee committees.

_____ 14B.   Employees should be part of the interviewing process for the hiring of additional *employees*.

_____ 15A.   Managers can be expected to resent having subordinates rate them. Managers should be rated by superiors.

_____ 15B.   Management should be periodically evaluated by workers on such dimensions as fairness, decision-making, objectivity, and knowledge of the job.

Fill in your scores below and total each column.

Boss Control	Subordinate Control
1B_____	1A_____
2A_____	2B_____
3A_____	3B_____
4B_____	4A_____
5B_____	5A_____
6A_____	6B_____
7B_____	7A_____
8A_____	8B_____
9A_____	9B_____
10B_____	10A_____
11B_____	11A_____
12A_____	12B_____
13A_____	13B_____
14A_____	14B_____
15A_____	15B_____
Total_____	Total_____

The two totals should add up to 150.

As you read on, these scores will be interpreted in terms of the model on the opposite page, which shows a simple framework for viewing the participation of boss and subordinate in the PRD process.

BOSS CONTROL

SUBORDINATE CONTROL

2. Boss
Appraises, then
Discusses

5. Boss and
Subordinate
Negotiate
the Appraisal

1. Boss Appraises

6. Subordinate
Appraises

3. Boss Discusses
then Appraises

4. Boss Solicits
Goals/Ratings,
then Appraises

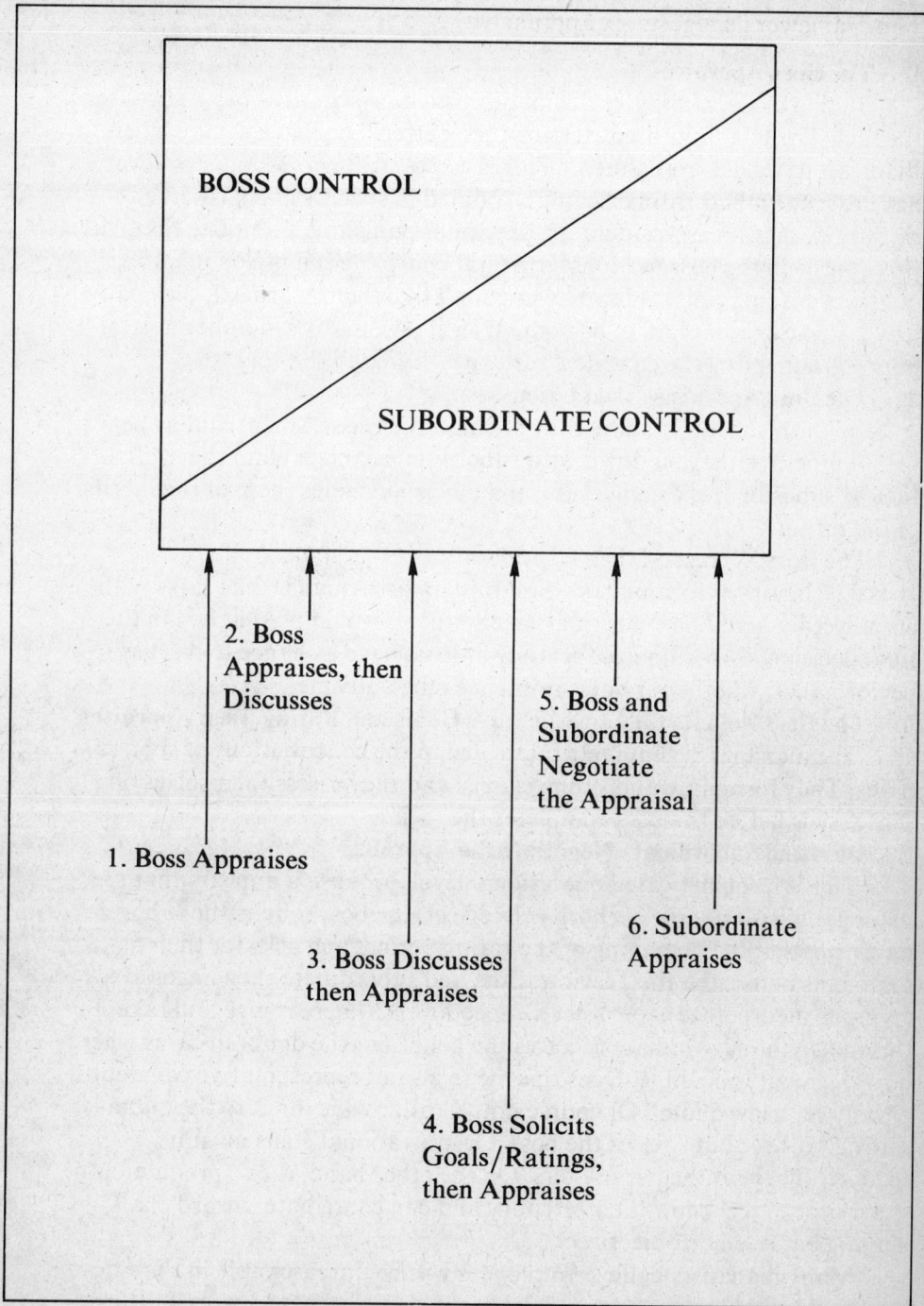

Continuum of PRD Boss-Subordinate Involvement

This framework suggests six approaches:

1. **The Boss Appraises**

   In this mode, managers do not discuss the assessment before or after the fact. The less subordinates know, the better. Feedback occurs when there is a paycheck adjustment. This is a safe strategy. Managers never have to justify their ratings, can't be pinned to specifics, and reserve the right to change an assessment for reward or punishment. Notice that with this approach the boss never asserts total control. Even prison inmates hold power (e.g., riots). If employees don't like their appraisal, they can leave, strike or complain to personnel; or, if a woman or member of a minority group, he or she can file a suit with EEO and the courts.

2. **The Boss Appraises, then Discusses**

   With this mode, managers are firm in their assessment, but as benevolent autocrats, they sit down with subordinates and explain the evaluation. If subordinates disagree, this manager persuades them of the merits of the rating.

3. **The Boss Discusses, then Appraises**

   The manager formulates a preliminary assessment, then talks with employees. Should new information emerge, it would be weighed in the final decision. Subordinates feel they at least have a chance to discuss performance, whether or not it influences the outcome.

4. **The Boss Solicits the Subordinate's Goals and Rating, then Appraises**

   The manager is genuinely interested in the contributions of subordinates. They formulate and submit goals, and they assess themselves on those goals before the boss completes the rating.

5. **Boss and Subordinate Negotiate the Appraisal**

   This is a sophisticated operational level, because it appears that the manager gives up some authority. In effect, the boss solicits the subordinates' goals at the beginning of the rating period, and asks for their assessments before the final review. Boss and subordinate then negotiate, trying to incorporate each other's expectations. There is give and take. In this mode, the subordinate receives the benefit of the doubt in cases where no agreement is possible. Does this mean a sales representative can deliberately set a low quota? Of course not. Reps provide input to the quota-setting process, but so does the boss. Organizational goals must be reached. They set the parameters. On the other hand, reps (production supervisors, etc.) know their territory and can contribute toward challenging but realistic objectives.

   Many managers believe employees will be unreasonable in their demands. There may be a certain irresistible logic in that view, but little evidence to support it. In practice, most subordinates act as reasonably and conscientiously as their bosses. We *must* believe this, since all of us are both boss *and* subordinate in our organizations.

6.   **The Subordinate Assesses**

In this extreme mode, subordinates complete a self-assessment, and, for the most part, that becomes final.

In which of the six modes do you operate? Since the statements 1A-15B are not scientifically validated, the scores approximate the degree to which you involve subordinates in the appraisal process.

Below the model is truncated to show a scale from the boss's view.

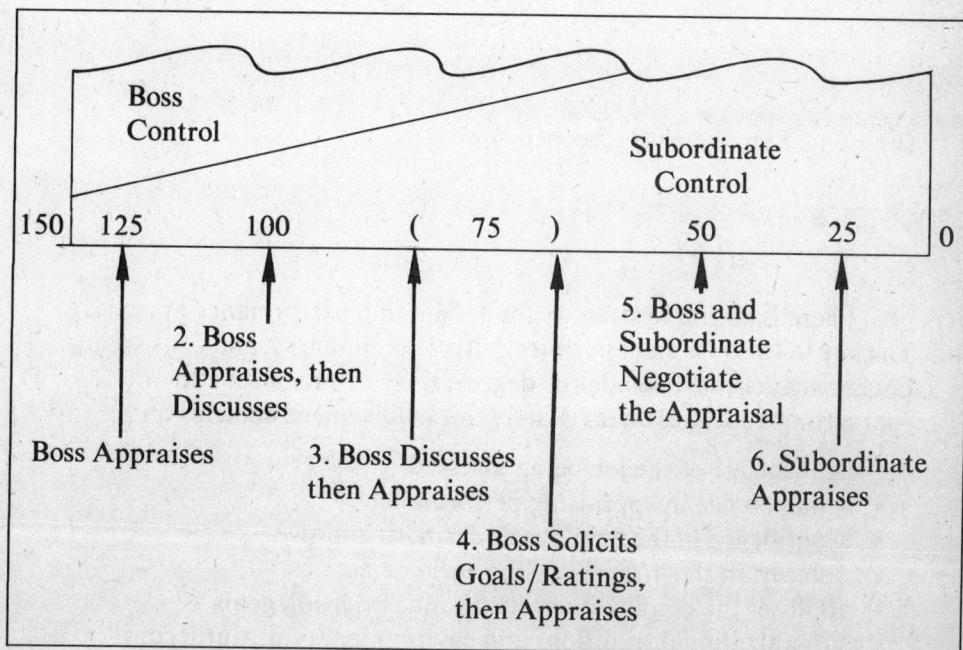

Since total control never occurs in the real world, scores of 150 or 0 are impossible. Match your Boss Control Score to the style below as a rough estimate of your feelings for or against involving subordinates in the appraisal process.

Involvement Style	Boss Control Score
1	125
2	100
3 }	75
4	
5	50
6	25

Which of the six modes are operating in your organization?

How would you change your appraisal practices to move one step up or down on the PRD Involvement Continuum?
(a)   One Step Up (more control):

(b)   One Step Down (less control):

There is no single strategy for conducting performance appraisals. The key to PRD is fairness, objectivity, thoroughness, and consistency. Each manager must decide the degree of involvement for subordinates in goal setting and assessment. Partly this involvement depends on:

- Knowledge of the job being assessed
- Competence in appraising performance
- Confidence in the employee's desire to improve
- Interest in short-term vs. long-term objectives
- Skills of the employee in setting and reviewing goals
- Organizational traditions and environment (e.g., authoritarian-democratic)

THE CASE FOR GREATER INVOLVEMENT
OF EMPLOYEES IN PRD

Modern bias leans toward greater involvement of subordinates for the following reasons:

- We are moving into a socio-political era begun in the late 60s, where people demand involvement in decisions affecting them. In the 80s, states will lean toward legislation favoring corporate employees, allowing them to see their personal files.
- PRD is designed for development, and development should occur when managers aren't around. Since employees will not sabotage their own enterprise, it makes sense that if we want them to upgrade their performance, they should help plan improvements.

- Motivation and a sense of responsibility come with participation. Group dynamics research suggests that members who are directly involved in the activities of the group tend to have a greater sense of responsibility and motivation to work toward group goals.
- Participating as a team promotes task execution. More and more employees suffer from anomie, a term coined by the French sociologist and philosopher, Émile Durkheim. It refers to a feeling of isolation and aloneness created by the size of institutions, burgeoning urbanization, increased specialization, and greater emphasis on complex technologies. Employees don't see the end result of their contributions, nor the consequences of their work. Involvement promotes a sense of belonging, a team spirit. When one does well, all benefit; when one underachieves, the entire department suffers. Commitments made in isolation are seldom kept. But when manager and employee resolve together, the chances of following through are greatly enhanced.
- Readiness for change is amplified. Change can be dictated, but implementing change cannot. Employees need to feel they will be able to perform under new conditions. They require support (training and resources) while adjusting to a changed state. Involvement in that adjustment promotes acceptance of new policies and procedures.
- Two-way dialogue is expanded. Implementing PRD, as discussed here, requires eliciting employees' viewpoints as well as feeding back the impressions of management. Disagreement and dissonances can be surfaced before they grow into major disputes.
- Emotions need a safety valve. When employees have no avenue for venting their frustrations, anger and resentment build and manifest themselves in poor workmanship, stoppages, improper use of time, and in some cases, sabotage. Participation in PRD acts as a safety valve and early warning system for diagnosing and solving problems.
- Personnel are more effectively utilized. One major dilemma is balancing organizational and individual goals so employees don't respond like robots, or, at the other extreme, fly off in all directions like popped corn. Much has been written about stimulating human potential, but little has been accomplished. Involving subordinates creates opportunities to discover ideas, strengths, and potentialities that might otherwise go unnoticed. If implemented jointly, PRD encompasses the ideas of employees as well as managers.

What are some kinds of involvement in PRD? First, there is the involvement of colleagues in defining the responsibilities of a job. Clarity and objectivity are directly related to how specifically the job is understood.

A second kind of involvement is seeking the views of others in gathering data. The more perspectives a manager gets, the greater the chance of completing a total picture of a subordinate's performance.

A few managers have subordinates rate *them*. I favor this procedure because it truly turns PRD into a two-way system, and can give managers insights into how their behaviors contribute to or hinder getting the job done. Warning: before experimenting with subordinate evaluations of your managing, make sure you can accept criticism without becoming defensive and reacting vindictively.

The advice and reactions of superiors represent a third kind of involvement. To avoid confusion, reach consensus on an appraisal with superiors before discussing it with the employee.

A final involvement, the one spotlighted in this chapter, occurs with the employees. It includes:

- Defining the job
- Setting mutual goals
- Systematically reviewing those goals throughout the year
- Conducting at least two formal review sessions, preceded by the subordinate's self-assessment

Interdependence between managers and employees in PRD matters has been stressed. A summary set of guidelines for encouraging and managing employee participation is presented here:

(a) Solicit employee ideas by asking open-ended questions.

(b) Listen actively, encouraging repeated employee contributions.

(c) Show understanding. Above all, avoid approving or disapproving statements. Be gracious; be receptive.

(d) Positively reinforce those ideas, activities, methods, or accomplishments that seem laudable. Subordinates care about and need praise.

(e) Probe for additional information. The best way to encourage further participation is to ask for examples or to question *"Why?"*

(f) Commit to further action. Ideally, this commitment would result in immediate use of some ideas suggested by employees. The least action would be to thank employees for their contribution, and schedule another session to discuss other topics. A key to involvement is the commitment to follow employee suggestions, and, where a recommendation cannot be enacted, at least provide an explanation.

Involvement demands follow-through and exchange. Giving and receiving feedback work best under the following principles:

- Time your feedback to the performance and the readiness of the employee; then it is most beneficial.
- Report the facts rather than suppositions about why things happened.
- Focus on new information, not only the obvious.
- Rather than demand fundamental changes in the employee, concentrate on job-related behaviors.

- Don't overload employees.
- Share enthusiasm (or concern) over the feedback.
- Identify preferred ways for the employee to react.
- Check what has been heard, rumored, or suggested.
- Let employees know when *their* feedback has been helpful. (See "Feed Back Negatives" on p. 142. Also discussed in the author's *Face-To-Face Communications,* Xicom Inc., 1973, pp. 102–103.)

Initially, the involvement of employees in PRD can be threatening. But those who try it usually find that most employees want to do the job well. They want to contribute, to feel a sense of efficacy. The growing size and complexity of organizations promotes alienation, and makes it difficult for employees to see their impact on the final product or service. Encouraging their participation in assessing work need not undermine your role as boss — you always wear that mantle. Involvement can create a sense of partnership. Managers have tried many things to increase productivity that have not worked. At least including employees in their appraisals is worth the trial.

What Do You Give Up?	What Do You Gain?
Some authority	Expanded power because subordinates are *assuming* more responsibility.
Some direct control	Employees with more self-control, who operate when you're not around.
Some efficiency	Greater effectiveness.
The image of "management mastery"	Substance and credibility.
One-way communication	Negotiations against the backdrop of organizational objectives.
Some surface comfort	Fewer frustrated subordinates.

Some Risks and Benefits of Involvement

Managing consent vs. the divine right of the boss has been a theme of this chapter. Two hundred years ago, George III didn't fare too well with his divine right. Representation is in the seams of U.S. history. In terms of PRD, expect low satisfaction to result from the employees' lack of power to participate in their own evaluations (Notion 17 in Chapter 1). And expect, if not low performance, certainly unimproved performance.

Approach involvement by degrees. Begin by *discussing* the assessment of performance. Next *ask employees to submit their goals*. Finally, when you feel that you and your subordinates can manage, enlist their self-assessments. In the end, your managerial judgment will prevail. In the meantime, employees may surprise you in the accuracy of their analyses, the quality and quantity of their ideas, and in their commitment to improve — the ultimate and sole justification for performance appraisal and the subject of the last chapter.

APPLICATION AND REVIEW

1. Cite six guidelines for encouraging employee involvement in the PRD interview:

    (a)

    (b)

    (c)

    (d)

    (e)

    (f)

2. Pick one of your employees and answer the following questions:

    (a) Do I know what expectations the employee holds for me?
    (b) How many times in the last month has the employee told me what he/she liked? Disliked?
    (c) Note two ways you can get more feedback from that employee:

        (1)

        (2)

    (d) Devise one technique for gaining greater employee involvement in her/his next appraisal.

3. Overheard in the hall:
    (a) "He says his door is always open but nobody gets in."
    (b) "She never asks our opinions."
    (c) "Have you ever tried to get by his secretary?"
    (d) "The only time I hear from him is when I'm in trouble."

    If they were your subordinates, how would you respond to each one?

4. (a) What are the six levels of involving employees in their appraisals?
    (a)

    (b)

    (c)

    (d)

    (e)

    (f)

5. Pick one subordinate and conceive a plan for his/her involvement in the next appraisal.

SUGGESTED RESPONSES

1. (a) Ask questions
   (b) Listen actively
   (c) Show understanding
   (d) Reinforce positives
   (e) Probe
   (f) Act

2. Responses will vary.

3. Responses will vary.

4. Boss appraises, boss appraises/discusses, boss discusses/appraises, boss solicits goals and rating/appraises, boss and subordinate negotiate the appraisal, subordinate appraises.

CHAPTER 12

TRANSLATING APPRAISALS INTO IMPROVED PERFORMANCE

"This is my career we're talking about. How does this appraisal affect it?"
"Isn't this tied to my raise?"
"You can't get blood out of a turnip."
"*You* tell me how to improve that!"
"You don't give us any support."
"I do my best. What do you want from me?"

We have placed heavy emphasis on *doing* and *communicating* skills at the expense of other human interactive processes. One observation is that most people fail in organizations for interpersonal rather than technical reasons. That is, they can't get along, their colleagues don't like them, they are antisocial, they destroy group morale, or they obstruct; they are too progressive, traditional, inflexible, gossipy, malicious, dishonest, anti-management, and so on. In addition to being technically accurate, PRD must be administered to account for the human conflicts inevitable in organizational life.

```
Define Job Responsibilities
            ↓
       Set Goals ←──────┐
            ↓           │
    Gather Information  │
            ↓           │
    Assess Performance  │
            ↓           │
Communicate That Assessment │
            ↓           │
Decide on a Course of Action ┘
```

Four concepts are worth considering in deciding on a course of action for improvement:

(a) *Energy*—the law for the *economy of energy* states that to the extent groups have worked out their interpersonal problems, they will have greater energy available for productive work. Poor face-to-face relationships force managers and employees to devote an inordinate

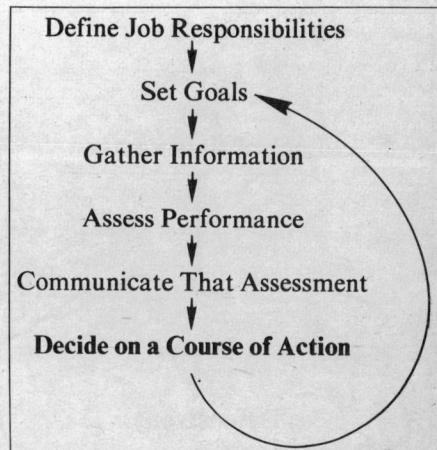

amount of time to problems of misunderstanding, lack of support, accusations, and miscommunication.

(b)   *Leveling*—failure to communicate honestly leads to a decrease in managerial credibility and a pattern of manager-to-employee transactions. In this one-way relationship, the employee's ideas have no way of getting out on the table for consideration.

(c)   *Anxiety*—distress caused by apprehension about one's work impedes effective action. Productivity calls for the full use of resources, and increases as the manager creates a climate of acceptance and support.

(d)   *Intentions*—"The best-laid plans of mice and men often go astray," said Robert Browning. In short, what we achieve is not always what we hope to accomplish. This gap between intention, actions, and effect must be continually bridged in PRD. Consider a case in which a manager, in assessing a supervisor's performance, determines that the number of products rejected by quality control is increasing rather than reducing. Two approaches to the problem are traced below. On the opposite page the interpersonal gap for the approach (a) is diagrammed.

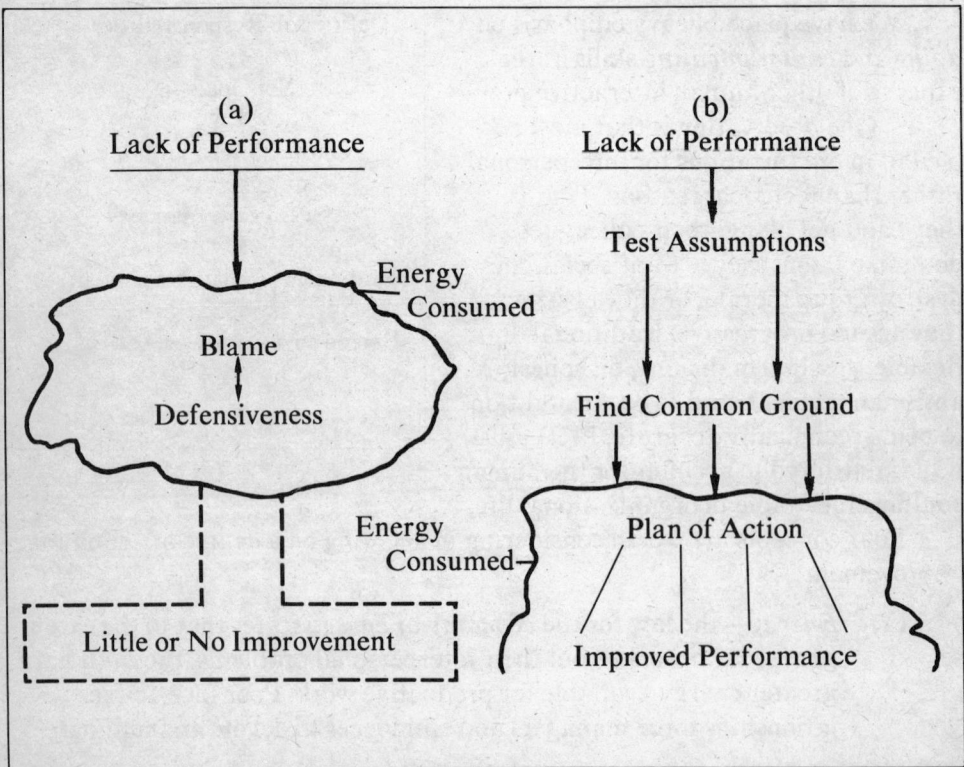

(a)
Lack of Performance

Energy Consumed

Blame

Defensiveness

Energy Consumed

Little or No Improvement

(b)
Lack of Performance

Test Assumptions

Find Common Ground

Plan of Action

Improved Performance

Two Reactions to Lack of Performance

Manager's Intention

There are too many rejects coming off the line. That must be corrected.

Manager's Action

"Barrett, what in the world is going on? Rejects are increasing. Aren't you on top of things down there?

(Blame)

Effect on Supervisor

"Sure, I am, but I got 100 things going on at once. I can't be everywhere. And besides, the people we hire don't know what they're doing."
(Defensiveness)

Supervisor's Inference About the Manager

"He's on me again. Whatta hardnose. Why doesn't he come down on the line and find out what I have to put up with."

Supervisor's Reaction

"I'm sorry. One of my best men has been out sick. That's probably the problem. It'll improve."

Supervisor's Intention

"I'm not going to get blamed for this one. I'll complain to Quality Control."

Manager's Inference About the Effect on the Supervisor.

I don't know why I have to yell to get something done, but it gets action. Now he'll get at the cause of the problem and correct it.

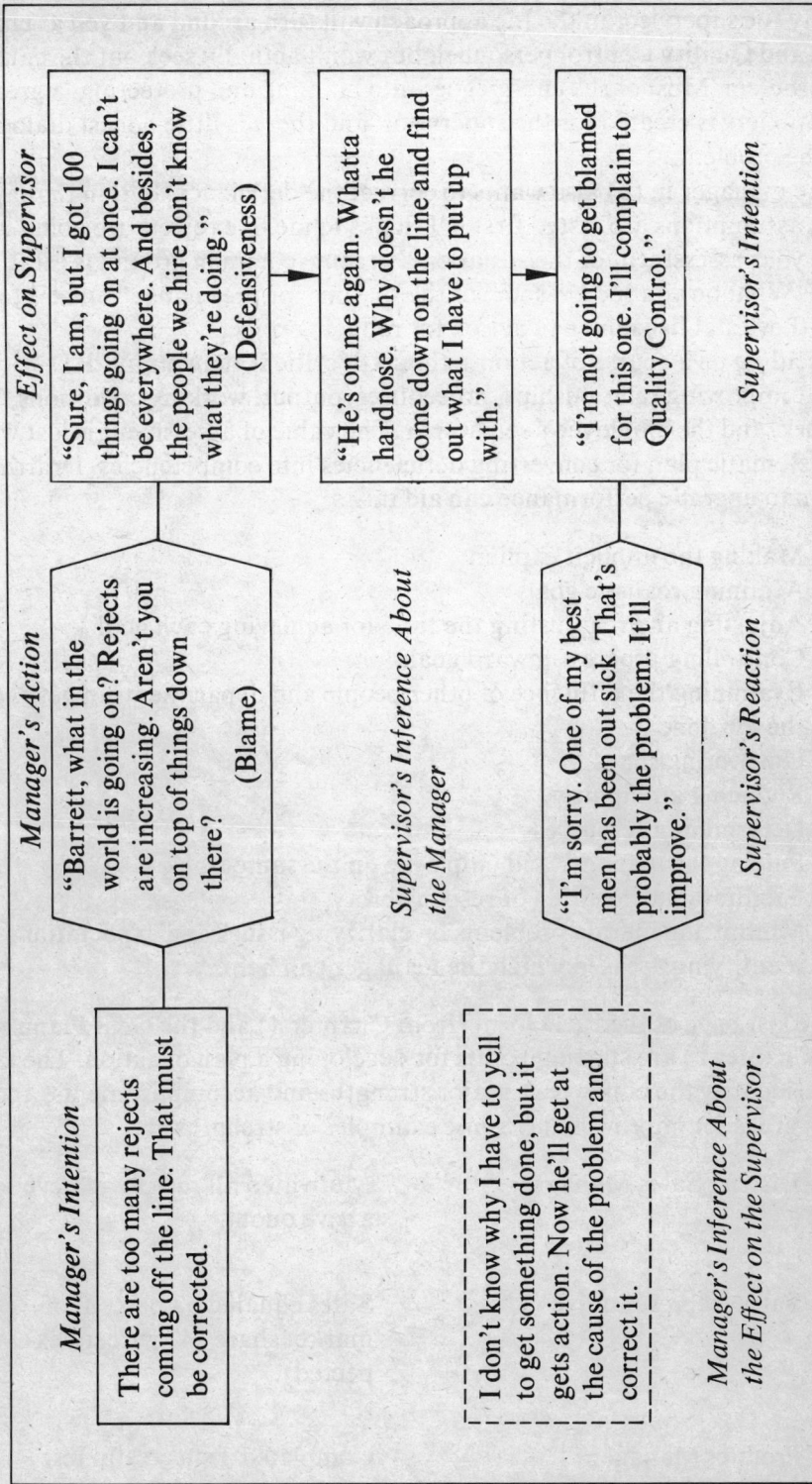

Note the gap between the manager's intention and the supervisor's interpretation of that intention. They do not match, nor does the manager's inference coincide with the supervisor's intention.

Probably the supervisor in the (a) approach will turn around and yell at employees and Quality Control personnel, but won't actually seek out the causes of the problem. Most of the energy goes into blaming and protecting, a great deal of anxiety is created for the supervisor, and there is little honest dialogue about the problem.

The manager in (b) also wants to correct the deficiency, but, in that approach, assumptions are tested first ("It looks to me like rejects are going up. What's your assessment of the situation?"); some common ground is established ("What do you see are some of the reasons for the change?"); and together, they establish a plan of action for reducing rejects.

Deciding on a course of action—the sixth critical element in PRD—is aimed at improving relationships, procedures, output, working conditions, teamwork, and the employee's self-worth. The value of assessment is lost without a systematic plan for converting deficiencies into competencies. Drafting a platform to upgrade performance can aid in:

- Making the implicit explicit
- Attaining realistic goals
- Adjusting and readjusting the time for achieving each goal
- Controlling progress toward goals
- Examining the influence of other people and departments in getting the job done
- Uncovering snags
- Reducing ambiguity
- Determining resources
- Putting the manager and employee on the same track
- Facilitating delegation of responsibility
- Minimizing morale problems by clarifying issues and expectations
- Identifying areas in which the manager can help.

The last page of the PRD form (from Chapter 4) and the Goal Planning Insert (Chapter 5) are starting points for developing a plan of action. The first step is to identify the employee's major strengths and accomplishments, and spell out areas for improvement. Some examples of strengths are:

— District Sales Manager	Motivated all reps to achieve above quota.
— Sales Representative	Sales equaled 53 percent of market share (47 percent expected).
— Product Manager	Completed 3 successful test market launches.

— Manager, Cost Accounting	Closing statements were accurate and timely.
— Plant Accountant	Periodically cross-trained all personnel.
— Design Engineer	Created new approaches to design problems, e.g., the hoist cylinder.
— Filling Department Head	Initiated and implemented a monthly safety program.
— Shift Supervisor	Reoperation was 5 percent under last year.

Listing the two or three areas where the employee needs to improve is actually a process of remodeling past purposes, of resetting goals. Establishing a program for improvement moves the employee away from thinking of unsatisfactory performance, toward "Where do we go from here?"

In setting up a plan, establish a list of priorities. Work first on the most significant, desired changes. These are advances that will result in a measurable improvement. George Morrisey, in *Getting Your Act Together* (John Wiley & Sons, Inc., 1980), suggests ordering priorities according to "got-to-do's, ought-to-do's, and nice-to-do's." Concentrate on the *got-to-do's.* Recognize that it is not necessary to deal with every problem in one performance review session. Improvement efforts frequently bog down as a result of attempting to cover too much.

Some suggested examples of "areas for improvement" include:

— **District Sales Manager**	Upgrade the presentations of the two reps with lowest sales.
	Improve distribution of "Big D" in 3 key accounts.
— **Sales Representative**	Follow up regularly with parts personnel.
	Hold expenses within budget.
	Submit a list of distributor personnel who lack product knowledge, and arrange for their training.

	Improve personal relationships with distributors X, Y and Z.
— Product Manager	Prevent time delays in the upcoming test market of our "Fresh Hair" shampoo.
— Manager, Cost Accounting	Initiate at least one cost saving procedure for manufacturing over the next 90 days.
— Plant Accountant	Learn how to do price variances.
— Design Engineer	Improve relations with manufacturing personnel by complimenting them when they do a good job and making them feel important.
— Filling Department Head	Keep up to date on schedule changes and adjust to meet them.
— Shift Supervisor	Maintain maximum (2 percent) regroup operations in assembly.
	Improve relations with standards department by initiating monthly communications with them.
	Maintain materials records to comply with usage system.

Even if the employee cannot agree whole-heartedly with your recommendations, some plan is better than none at all. *In medias res* said Horace: "Start with action."

In planning for development, ask the following questions:

- Is the action step DO-ABLE? Can it be accomplished by the people and resources available?
- What will be the IMPACT of the action on quantity, quality, cost, scheduling, and output? Is it really important?
- Is the action step specific? Does it spell out WHAT is to be done and WHEN it is to be completed?
- Is the accomplishment of the action step MEASURABLE? How will we evaluate the effort?
- What specific commitments can I make to SUPPORT and assist the employee?

The next page presents a 90-120 day Follow-Through Worksheet, which can be used along with the Goal Planning Insert (Chapter 5). The selected goals should be identified and discussed with the employee. In addition, spell out how each goal is to be achieved and how it will be measured. Finally, determine what help the subordinate needs to accomplish the goals. Give the employee a copy of the worksheet and agree on a time when another conference can be called to assess progress.

WORKSHEET

90-120 DAY FOLLOW-THROUGH OF IMPROVEMENT STEPS

Employee's Name _____

I.   Selected Improvement Goals:

 1. _____
 2. _____
 3. _____

II. Methods for achieving each improvement (Use additional
     pages as needed):

 1. _____
 2. _____
 3. _____

III. Deadline for each improvement and evidence that it has been
     reached:

     When?   How Measured?

 1. _____
 2. _____
 3. _____

IV. Support and resources needed to accomplish the improve-
     ments:

 1. _____
 2. _____
 3. _____

V.   Next review to check progress _____.
                                   (date)

Three important tactics to keep in mind:

(1)   *Checkpoints* — Establish indicators, as well as dates, for measuring ups and downs in performance.

(2)   *Error Detection* — Since for the most part we don't self-correct, managers must trouble-shoot, diagnose, and provide the pillar and push for employee improvement.

(3)   *Reinforcement* — Reward, reward, reward! We have grossly ignored and under-used recognition as a motivational tool. The subordinate's lament: "The only time I hear from you is when I'm in trouble!" Reinforcing desired behaviors can go a long way in any improvement plan.

> "You gotta accentuate the positive and
> eliminate the negative!"

Summarizing improvement ideas from this and previous chapters, here are six guidelines to keep in mind when constructing a blueprint for development:

• Target one or two areas—don't try to cover too much. A serious mistake managers make is to attempt to improve everything at once. When we consider our own development, it's hard enough to work on one or two areas, not to mention five or six.

• Determine the practicality of the goals for improvement—is it reasonable and realistic to believe that the employee can reach the goals? What will be the consequences if the goals are accomplished? If not accomplished? If little impact, then perhaps the goals aren't worth the time and effort.

• Spell out action steps—together with the employee, map out a stratagem specific enough for everyone to understand. Review the options in order not to straight-jacket the employee into one way of accomplishing the job.

• Establish deadlines—set specific dates to accomplish and review the developmental goals. Without deadlines, most work would not be completed.

• Identify how the development will be measured—ask "How will we know when the goal is accomplished? What will be different? What will have to be changed? What will the outcome look like?" Employees need to know how they will be measured so they can assess their own progress and make adjustments when necessary.

• Discuss ways employees can be supported—the manager's role is the keystone to development. Growth doesn't occur in a vacuum. We all need ideas and resources to assist in our own renewals.

How far to Robinson's farm?

Mile and a half.

How far is it to Robinson's farm?

'Bout a mile and a half.

How far to Robinson's farm?

A mile and a half.

Well, at least I'm holding my own.

Performance Review and Development, or any effective appraisal process, takes time and thought. Implementing PRD begins with specifying the job and setting goals, and ends with new or remodeled targets. PRD requires mutual understanding of expectations and of the criteria for determining the fulfillment of those expectations. Assessing performance is not an easy task; sometimes the pacing is two steps forward and one back. But preparation, openness and honesty will do much to compensate for PRD complexities.

Most managers understand the importance of maintaining equipment through the daily, preventive measures of line personnel and the periodic checkups made by maintenance. Similarly, our human systems need to be coaxed, cajoled, stroked, regenerated, and adjusted periodically. If subordinates regress after a review, don't be surprised. Equipment often breaks down thirty days after an overhaul.

Great social movements like religion build periodic renewals into their forecasts, e.g., weekly church revivals. Bridging intentions with behavior is an eternal struggle for humankind. In lieu of a continuing agenda for improvement, the gap will naturally widen.

So *HOW* does a performance appraisal lead to greater productivity? The answer rests in the interplay of technique (the data, the form, the measurement, the rating) and the manager's face-to-face employment of the system.

About answers, e.e. cummings once wrote, "Always the beautiful answer which asks a more beautiful question." The answers in this book ask: HOW DO YOU ...

— evaluate your subordinates' worth?
— help subordinates define and reach goals?
— stimulate enthusiasm for excellence?
— facilitate work by providing information, materials and assistance?
— establish minimum standards for performance?
— clarify and simplify procedures?
— gather information "on the run"?
— understand the dynamics of evaluation and the relationship between criteria, weighting, measurement, and rating?
— reach consensus on the job and its major responsibilities?
— create dialogue with subordinates about performance?
— reinforce positives and translate negatives into restoration?
— resolve the natural disagreements inherent in any working relationship?
— distinguish between results and methods?
— keep open to suggestions and ideas?

and, above all,
HOW do you reserve time for appraisals?

A successful appraisal process must provide for immediate adjustment when performance slackens. The payoff of those adjustments depends on the skills and insights of its participants. The *how* of appraisals and the *what* are synergetic. They feed on each other. The result can be greater productivity as diagramed below.

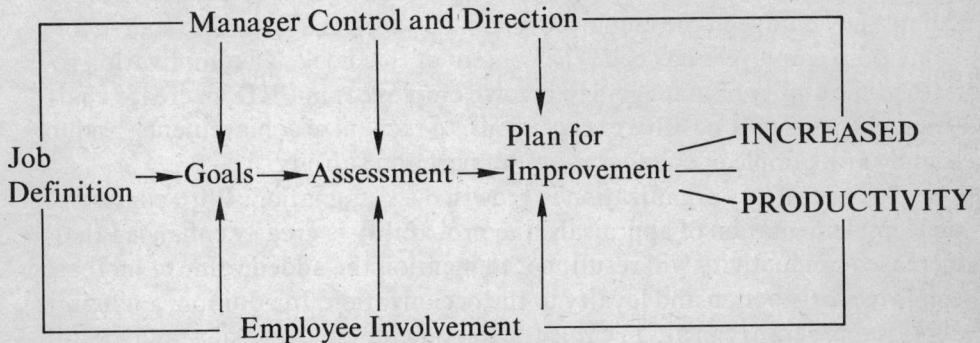

```
          ┌──────── Manager Control and Direction ─────────┐
          │             │              │           │        │
          │             ↓              ↓           ↓        │
Job       │                                    Plan for    ⌐ INCREASED
Definition├→ Goals ──→ Assessment ──→ Improvement ─
          │       ↑              ↑              ↑    ⌐ PRODUCTIVITY
          │       │              │              │        │
          └──────────── Employee Involvement ───────────┘
```

An organization derives its value from PRD through managers who implement it, and their spirit, skill and commitment to it as a way to improve productivity. The appraisal's significance depends on:

• HOW management supports it

- HOW adequately you can separate PRD from salary considerations
- HOW job related it is
- HOW goal-oriented you are
- HOW successful you are in upgrading your skills and techniques in administering PRD
- HOW willing and adept you are at involving employees in their own development
- HOW willing and skilled employees are in their self-improvement efforts

And, if your subordinates are also managers who appraise employees, the success of PRD depends on your ability and willingness to criticize their assessments. A guide to upgrading the appraisals of managers reporting to you is outlined in the Appendix.

I have tried throughout the book to surface the difficulties of appraising, and to propose ideas and procedures for managing them. The thrust has been moving from form filling to franchising the potential of employees for greater productivity. If implemented diligently, PRD can improve managing as well as employee performance. Serious appraising will increase the quantity and quality of ideas, improve methods (reducing costs), and increase the production of employees (greater revenues, increased production). And that, you will recall, results in greater productivity. Obviously, there are a multitude of variables affecting productivity, but I am suggesting one—the appraisal process—that is within the manager's control.

Organizations suffer from dry rot—piles of mediocre work never rectified. Managers cannot continue to whitewash poor performance in the name of compensation or staying on the "good side" of subordinates. Nor should they bludgeon the employee who falls short. A systematic course for motivating employees has been the content of this book. That motivation relates to the ability of managers to involve employees in PRD, to create challenging goals, to set positive expectations, to recognize achievements, and to lead by an example of collaboration, support and subsidy.

The aim of any organization is growth over stagnation. With conscientious implementation of appraisals, the probability is greatly enhanced that increased productivity will result, not to mention the added value of increased employee satisfaction and loyalty to the organization. In addition, a dynamic appraisal program can aid in career development, job expansion, and identification of management potential. It is the core process for developing talent and mining the "people" potential within the organization.

The option to PRD, and to any disciplined appraisal practice, is stargazing. Frankly, I'll put my money on planned, caring procedures. The stars are too far away and even *they* fall.

APPLICATION AND REVIEW

1. Identify five benefits of planning with employees for improvement:

   (a)

   (b)

   (c)

   (d)

   (e)

2. Six general guidelines for constructing a plan are:

   (a)

   (b)

   (c)

   (d)

   (e)

   (f)

3. Using your appraisal system and forms, follow the guidelines in this and preceding chapters to draft a blueprint for improvement with one of your subordinates. Try to define its specific impact on productivity, either by increasing output (effectiveness) or decreasing the costs of input (efficiency).

4. If your subordinates are managers who appraise their employees, review their recent assessments using the checklist in the Appendix.

5. *Economy of energy* refers to:

SUGGESTED RESPONSES

1.   A plan helps to reach realistic goals, make the implicit explicit, adjust deadlines, control progress, examine others' influence on the job, uncover snags, reduce ambiguity, and determine resources.

2.   (a)   Target one or two areas
     (b)   Determine practicality
     (c)   Spell out actions
     (d)   Establish deadlines
     (e)   Identify measurement procedures
     (f)   Support the employee's efforts

3.   Responses will vary.

4.   Responses will vary.

5.   Managers and employees focusing their energies on the job rather than on bickering, blame, and defensiveness.

AFTERWORD

"Hi, Jerry, good to see you. Have a seat. Boy, I want you to know I really appreciate that report you got to me on how to improve our distribution. There are ideas in there we can implement immediately. I'm convinced it's really going to help."

WARM-UP

"Yeah, you think so? That's good to hear."

"Did you have a chance to do some preparation for your appraisal?"

PREPARATION

"Yeah, I appreciate your giving me these questions to consider two weeks ago, so I could jot down some of my ideas."

"Well, good, and I've blocked out two hours with no appointments. I've told Marion not to put through any calls. So I'm ready to go. It may only take 20 minutes, but at least the time is there if we need it."

SCHEDULING

"I appreciate that, because most of the time you're going one way and I'm going another. It's these rare times you plan with me that are really helpful."

"We're all busy, but I try to make sure we get together at least four times a year to sit down and talk about how things are going. That doesn't always happen in our day-to-day and week-to-week discussions where we're usually dealing with some crisis. I just hope I've given you my feedback as things have happened or not happened throughout the year, so they'll be no surprises today."

CONTINUITY

"I think I have a pretty good picture of where I stand."

"O.K. Let's just quickly review the job responsibilities that you and I agreed on."

CLARIFYING THE JOB

(They review the responsibilities and agree on their importance.)

"I think we're pretty much in agreement on what the job is. Let's review how we did on the goals you and I set back in January and revised in June. Why don't you give me your assessment!

REVIEWING GOALS

"O.K., I'll go right down the list. Of the ten goals, I believe I accomplished eight. One was not accomplished, and one I don't think we can determine at this time. Let me give you my reasons for rating the goals this way."

EMPLOYEE PARTICIPATION

(He discusses each goal.)

"Hey, you've been very thorough in your analysis, Jerry, and you've brought up some points I hadn't thought of. I want you to know I realize what you've accomplished."

REINFORCEMENT

(Boss now goes on to list those accomplishments he concurs with, and others Jerry hasn't mentioned.)

"Now, there's one I'm not quite sure of, Jerry. That's the goal relating to improving relationships with our biggest customers. Let me give you some of the problems I see there." (Boss elaborates.) "How do you feel about that?"

AREAS FOR IMPROVEMENT

"Well, I thought I did a pretty good job, but I can see your point. That could be improved, I suppose."

(Give and take continues. Boss clarifies position on other goals, then gives his analysis of Jerry's total performance ending with the overall rating.)

RATING

"Well, frankly, I kind of think of myself as outstanding. I'm a little disappointed in the rating of *excellent,* although I know that places me above most of my colleagues."

"How about the three problem areas I mentioned, Jerry? What do you see we can do to improve those?"

"Well, in the customer relations one, I think probably I could make a point to call on the five major accounts every month." (etc.)

(Boss gives his ideas on what can be done and together they agree on a strategy.)

PLAN FOR IMPROVEMENT

"O.K., what I've done is written down our revised goals, Jerry, and how we'll know when we reach them. What do you say we get together in, let's see . . . Christmas is a mess and January we're just getting started in our new programs . . . How about getting together in February to take a look at our progress?"

GOAL SETTING

"That sounds O.K."

"Now, what can I do to assist you in these areas?"

SUPPORT

"Well, for one it'd be helpful if you could come along with me to one of our major accounts."

"O.K., why don't I plan to do that early in January? You set it up and let me know the date. Also, how about on this whole organizing-your-work-bit, why don't we make sure, in the next three months, that we get you off to a seminar on time management."

"Sure, but you know those seminars—they usually aren't much help."

"We'll see if we can find a good one, O.K.? We've been going at it now for more than an hour. Do you have any other comments or questions? What needs further clarification?"

"Well, no, in general I think it's gone pretty well. We have some minor disagreements, but I understand your point of view and I also know what needs to be done."

"I don't expect we'll agree all the time, Jerry, but frankly, if we disagree, we ought to understand each other's position, and I'll remain open to new data that would alter my thinking. Why don't you summarize your understanding of the appraisal and where we go from here?"

DEALING WITH DISAGREEMENT

CHECKING FOR UNDERSTANDING

"O.K., my strengths are . . . (he enumerates) Some areas I'm going to work on are . . . " (he reviews new goals and deadlines)

"That's the way I see it, too, and I feel

WRAP-UP

good about this review. You've done a fine job. It's been a good year, and I'm looking forward to an even better one next year. You're one of my best people, so hang in there. Let me know anytime you don't think I'm giving you the feedback you need to do the job."

"You can be sure I'll do that."

"O.K. Here, you take the copy of what we've said and what we've committed ourselves to. I'll plan to travel with you after the holidays and then—why don't we say February 21st— we'll get together to see where we're at. O.K.?

DOCUMENTATION

SET NEXT REVIEW

"O.K."

"Thanks for coming in, Jer. Are you and the family going anywhere over the holidays?"

"Yeah, we're going up to my folks in Wisconsin."

"Well, take care."

Record of a Performance
Appraisal of Jerry, Conducted at
Metropolitan Products Inc. (MPI)
December, 1981

BIBLIOGRAPHY

(Useful sources not cited in the text.)

"Assessment Centers." *Personnel Administration*. February, 1980.

Beer, Michael and Robert A. Ruh. "Employee Growth Through Performance Management." *Harvard Business Review*. July-August, 1976.

Burke, Ronald J. "Why Performance Appraisal Systems Fail." *Personnel Administration*. May-June, 1972.

Danzig, Selig M. "What We Need to Know About Performance Appraisals." *Management Review*. February, 1980.

Dornbusch, Sanford M. and W. Richard Scott. *Evaluation and the Exercise Of Authority*. Jossey-Bass Publishers, San Francisco, California, 1975.

"Evaluation Techniques." *Training and Development Journal*. October, 1980. Includes the following articles:

Beaulieu, Rod. "An Easier Look At Performance Appraisal."

Hamelink, Jack and Jerry. "A Numeric Plan For Performance Appraisal."

Hersey, Paul and Marshall Goldsmith. "The Changing Role of Performance Management."

Putnam, Anthony O. "Pragmatic Evaluation."

Gallagher, Michael C. "More Bias In Performance Evaluation?" *Personnel*. July-August, 1978.

Lambert, Clark. *Field Sales Performance Appraisal*. John Wiley & Sons, Inc., New York, 1979.

Lazer, Robert I. "Performance Appraisal: What Does The Future Hold?" *Personnel Administrator*. July, 1980.

Lefton, R. E. and V. R. Buzzotta. "Performance Appraisal: Why Bother?" *Training and Development Journal*. August, 1978.

Mager, Robert F. and Peter Pipe. *Analyzing Performance Problems or "You Really Oughta Wanna."* Fearon Publishers, Inc., Belmont, California, 1970.

Maier, Norman R. F. *The Appraisal Interview, Three Basic Approaches*. University Associates, Inc., La Jolla, California, 1976.

Mathis, Robert L. and Richard H. Sutton. "Performance Appraisal—Part 1." *Journal of Systems Management*. V.30, No. 6, June, 1979. and "Part 2." V.30, No. 7, July, 1979.

National Retail Merchants Association, Personnel Division. *Measuring Executive and Employee Performance: Updating Appraisal Methods*. New York, 1970.

Odiorne, George S. *Management by Objectives*. Pitman Publishing Corporation, New York, 1965.

Odiorne, George S. *Management by Objectives II*. Fearon Pitman Publishers Inc., Belmont, California, 1979.

Patz, Alan L. "Performance Appraisal: Useful But Still Resisted." *Harvard Business Review*. May-June, 1975.

"Performance Appraisal Series." Reprint from *Harvard Business Review*. No. 21143, 1972. Includes the following articles:

Flanagan, John C. and Robert K. Burns. "The Employee Performance Record."

Kelly, Philip R. "Reappraisal Of Appraisal."

Kindall, Alva F. and James Gatza. "Positive Program For Performance Appraisal."

Lasagna, John B. "Make Your MBO Pragmatic."

Levinson, Harry. "Management By Whose Objectives?"

Mayfield, Harold. "In Defense Of Performance Appraisal."

McGregor, Douglas. "An Uneasy Look At Performance Appraisal."

Meyer, H.H., E. Kay, and J.R.P. French, Jr. "Split Roles In Performance Appraisal."

Oberg, Winston. "Make Performance Appraisal Relevant."

Sloan, Stanley and Alton C. Johnson. "New Context Of Personnel Appraisal."

Thompson, Paul H. and Gene W. Dalton. "Performance Appraisal: Managers Beware."

White, Frank B. and Louis B. Barnes. "Power Networks in the Appraisal Process."

Reider, George A. "Performance Appraisal—A Mixed Bag." *Harvard Business Review*. July-August, 1973.

Schwab, Donald P., Herbert G. Heneman, III, and Thomas A. DeCotiis, "Behaviorally Anchored Rating Scales: A Review of the Literature." *Personnel Psychology*. Winter, 1975.

Smith, Howard P. and Paul J. Brouwer. *Performance Appraisal and Human Development. A Practical Guide to Effective Managing*. Addison-Wesley Publishing Co., Reading, Massachusetts, 1977.

Tosi, Henry L., John R. Rizzo, and Stephen J. Carroll. "Setting Goals in Management by Objectives." *California Management Journal*. V.12, No. 4, Summer, 1970.

Winstanley, N. B. "How Accurate Are Performance Appraisals?" *Personnel Administration*. August, 1980.

Winstanley, N. B. "Legal and Ethical Issues in Performance Appraisals." *Harvard Business Review*. November-December, 1980.

VideoTape Program: "5 PA Modules." R. Fischer Olson & Assoc., Inc., Woodland, Cedar Lane, Ossining, N.Y. 10562.

APPENDIX

A CHECKLIST FOR UPGRADING THE QUALITY OF THE PERFORMANCE APPRAISALS CONDUCTED BY YOUR MANAGERS

APPRAISAL ANALYSIS CHECKLIST

A Suggested List of Questions You May Wish to Consider As You Review and Analyze Appraisals Completed by Your Managers.

1. Are all parts of the appraisal form satisfactorily completed?
2. Does the appraisal give you a picture of the employee's performance?
3. Are the comments and examples specific enough?
4. Does the overall rating follow from the subratings?
5. Does the appraiser weigh any one item or factor so heavily that it inappropriately distorts the overall rating?
6. If you compare this appraisal with others by this appraiser, is there a pattern, e.g., a tendency to rate consistently low? High? Average?
7. Does the manager present the necessary information for you to make a decision regarding employee development, promotion, transfer, or termination?
8. On the scale below, rate (circle one number) the written assessment:

Unclear   1   2   3   4   Thorough
Not specific   ├──┼──┼──┤   Clear
Incomplete   Substantiated

9. Are areas for improvement stated specifically enough so that a plan for improvement can be developed? For example, "needs to improve attitude" is too general. A more specific statement would be: "Once a decision is made, this employee needs to support and carry it out, even if he disagrees with the decision."

Return the written assessment to the appraiser for any of the following reasons:

    (a) You rated the appraisal below "3" in question 8.
    (b) You answered "no" to questions 1, 2, 3, 4, or 7.
    (c) You responded "yes" to questions 5 or 6.
    (d) The evaluation is outdated.

When returning the written assessment, indicate what additional information, supportive evidence, and clarification you need in order to take further action.

Suggested Questions for Consideration if You Choose to Hold a Telephone or Face-To-Face Discussion with the Appraiser.

1. Are job responsibilities identified, and are they the most significant responsibilities associated with the position?
2. Are there any others that you would consider major? Why?
3. Are the goals specified, and do you consider them important to the job?
4. Give examples of specific job behaviors for each rating level (outstanding, competent, etc.). Are these examples of performance level realistic? Too harsh? Too lenient?
5. If you question a rating or sub-rating, ask the appraiser to give examples of the employee's work that substantiate the rating.
6. Are the examples cited in the appraisal one-time happenings? Repeated behaviors? Consistent with what you know of the employee?
7. What specific strengths or weaknesses contributed most to the overall appraisal?
8. In those areas identified as needing improvement:
    What is the employee doing to correct them?
    What are you doing to support and assist him/her?
    How are you going to measure the improvement?
9. If the employee evaluated is a top performer, how are you going to make use of the employee's strengths?
10. To what extent does the employee agree with your assessment?

Index